Dedicated to my friends from Bainbridge Junior High who attended from 1962 to 1964. Special thanks to my friend Cheryl and to my sister Susy who jogged my memory and gave me the courage to share my story. I am deeply grateful to my daughter Angela who has given many hours to proof my work and to believe that my story is worth telling.

TOSSING TO AND FRO'

The Coming of Age

Victoria Farnsworth

A NOTE FROM THE AUTHOR

This memoir depicts my life during the years I was in junior high school. The names of some people have been changed if I did not have their permission to use them in this book. The experiences related in the following chapters are written as I perceived them; how they affected me personally. I learned so much during this time of my life. I hope you will enjoy yourselves as you revisit with me and remember your own coming of age.

TABLE OF CONTENTS

A Note from the Author v

Preface ix

Warren Comes Home 1

A Course is Set 6

A Working Girl 9

Puppy Love 18

Junior High 24

A Storm to Remember 31

Old Cider 37

Home, Sweet Home 41

Smoking...45

The Christmas Parka 48

Stolen Kiss 53

Rockin' Around the Clock 58

Seventh-Grade Mixer..62

The Church Moves..67

Half Way Through 70

Coed Camp 74

More Trouble on the Water 79

Big Kids on the Block 85

That Infamous Day 91

The Birds 101

Here We Go Again 107

What's a Mormon? 112

Eighth-Grade Graduation 116

Summer Fun 122

Good-bye 130

Epilogue 139

About the Author 141

PREFACE

L ife was extremely chaotic during the spring and summer of 1962. Changing beds, supplying fresh towels, cleaning, washing, ironing, how much could two people do? Running a motel during the Seattle World's Fair was not an easy task. It really was too much for my mother and me; she got help and I got some freedom! However, with all the rapid changes in my life, I felt somewhat like I was on a ship, sailing stormy seas, tossing to and fro'.

I was looking forward to the end of summer and going into junior high school. It would mean I would see all of my friends from Wilkes School again, plus the added bonus of being with my new friends from McDonald School. I was forever getting ahead of myself and looking toward to the future. School hadn't even let out for the summer, only a few more days to go. . .

CHAPTER 1

WARREN COMES HOME

School was going to be out in a few more days; I could hardly wait. As I was walking home from the bus stop, I was planning how my summer days would be spent. I would spend the early part of the days changing linens and scouring bathrooms. I would also help with the washing and ironing. But my afternoons would be totally mine, and I planned to make the most of them! I was envisioning Kitten and me getting into all sorts of fun trouble and, of course, having my friend Cheryl over to accompany us in whatever adventures came our way.

As I approached our apartments, I noticed a gray truck parked in front of our space. I figured it was some guest who had just arrived to stay during their visit to Century 21 (the Seattle World's Fair). I opened the kitchen door and walked into the house. I could hear deep voices and loud laughter coming from the living room. I walked through the makeshift hallway that joined our two apartments, and to my complete surprise, there was my brother Warren, my father, and a friend of theirs!

I gasped in amazement and could not say anything for a moment. I was so happy to see Warren and so embarrassed to let him and our father see me looking like such a mess. It was a warm day, and I knew I must look as disheveled as I felt. (I was at an age where I thought everyone noticed everything about my appearance.) I hoped Warren was home to stay, but maybe he was only here to see Century 21.

My father stood up and introduced himself. I managed to find my voice and told him that I knew who he was. I remembered him from when he came to take Warren to California to live. Warren interjected that he had come back to live with us; I about fell over right there!

My mother, of course, was also in the room, but I hadn't really noticed her. I was completely overwhelmed by the presence of my brother and father. The other man, who had come with them, stayed very quiet and did his best to stay out of the reunion and the conversation. Mom was thrilled that Warren had come home. She said that he could sleep in David's room, next to my room. David decided that he would move into the bedroom shared by my little brothers, Mike and Percy. Right there, in that instant, David grew up in my eyes. He went from a little brother, to an equal. How mature of him to give up his room for Warren. (I think he may have remembered past problems with Warren.)

Warren seemed different than when he had lived with us before. He certainly was much older and a lot nicer. He would be turning sixteen in September, so I guess he was old enough to control his emotions. He was anxious to get together with his old buddies from Seabold. I felt bad for him that he was stuck in Fort Ward at the south end of Bainbridge Island; it was a long way to walk or hitchhike. I said as much and he said he was sure some of his friends had cars or had parents who would let them borrow their cars. I glanced at Mom and saw the look of fear on her face. I knew she wasn't going to let Warren borrow her car.

My father and his friend were going to visit Century 21. Mom had a vacancy, so they settled themselves into an apartment, and I helped settle Warren into his room. Warren did not stick around for very long; he was on the phone calling old friends as soon as his bags were unpacked. He was so excited! It brought a lump to my throat and tears to my eyes to watch his antics while he was talking on the phone with his friends. He could not contain his complete joy and enthusiasm. After his last phone call, he said his friends were coming to get him and he would not be with us for dinner.

My father began to object but Mom said it was fine; he hadn't seen his friends in three and a half years. Warren was humming as he went to his room to change his clothes. I followed him and stood outside his doorway. I still was having a hard time believing he was really there. When he asked me what I was staring at, I replied that I was just so happy to see him. Then I asked the question that had been on my mind from the moment I first saw him, "What was it like living with our father?"

He told me that it wasn't so bad. He said that "Papi" (as he called him) was at work most of the time and that our great aunt looked out for him. He pretty much was on his own; Papi really didn't know much about being a father. Warren had been wanting to come home for a long time. He promised that he would be good and not tease or torment us as he had when he was younger. My brother seemed so sincere; I wanted, with all my heart, to believe him.

I decided that I needed to freshen myself up for dinner because my father and his friend would be joining us. My mother had given me lots of her old tubes of Avon lipstick from when she was a distributor. I hadn't used them for real, only in play. Since I had gotten older, I had only used them for Halloween. I certainly had never put any on to impress someone! However, at that moment, I decided I needed to look my best. I thought that a little lipstick would add some color to my face and make me look more mature. So I found a nice, dark pink color, and applied it to my lips. I used a piece of toilet tissue to blot them, and I thought that I looked quite nice. I went into the kitchen to see what I could do to help.

My father and his friend were sitting at the little table in the kitchen talking with my mother while she was preparing dinner. My dad wasn't home from work yet; I wondered how he was going to take all of this. I asked Mom what she would like me to do. She glanced at me and her eyes zoomed in on my lips and she exclaimed, "Oh My God! Why are you wearing lipstick?"

I fumbled for the words, totally embarrassed in front of my father. "I just wanted to look nice," was all I could manage to reply. My mother told me to march right into the bathroom and remove it immediately! I felt so humiliated; I couldn't understand why my mother had made such a fuss over a little lipstick. Good grief. I was almost thirteen years old!

As I walked by my father, he said very quietly, "I think it looks really nice." That made me feel better, and I went into the bathroom and gazed in the mirror wondering why I had to remove it. I thought about when Grandma had been here a few weeks earlier and Mom had told her that I wanted to wear a training bra. Grandma had laughed and said to me, "You've got nothing more than two pimples on a board!" I had been humiliated then too. I guess I cared too much about what people thought.

After washing my face, I went out into the dining room and set the table. I helped Mom in silence, not knowing what to say. I didn't want to interrupt her conversation with my father and his friend, and yet I had a billion questions to ask him. I just kept them bottled up inside me, hoping that I would have the opportunity to talk with him before he went back to California.

Dad came home from work, just in time for supper, as he did every weeknight. However, this time instead of smiles and his quiet, good-natured humor, he was shocked. Really, he walked through the door and his mouth dropped open! He collected his wits immediately and reached out and shook hands with my father and his friend, but I could tell that he was not pleased. My father sat next to me during dinner, and my dad was at the head of the table. I looked around at my younger brothers and sister; they could not keep their eyes off my father. My mother kept up her constant chatter, which she always did when she was nervous. The whole situation felt uncomfortable; I just wanted the meal to be over and for us to get on with our normal activities. I didn't have any homework because it was so close to the end of the year. My plans and daydreams of a few hours earlier had suddenly diminished and now paramount in my mind was figuring out a way to have a private conversation with my father. Then, if I was fortunate enough to get his undivided attention, what would I say? What questions would I ask, knowing that I probably would never have such an opportunity again? I pondered those thoughts as I fell asleep that night.

CHAPTER 2

A COURSE IS SET

The next morning Warren and I talked while I was getting ready for school. He had had a really fun reunion with his old buddies and was so happy to be home. He didn't know if he was going to the fair with our father and his friend. Warren just wanted to look around Fort Ward and explore. I wanted to stay home from school and show him around, but I knew I needed to be at school; there was so much going on this time of the year.

David, Susy, and I took off right after breakfast. We didn't have much to say to each other; the previous day's events still had all of us overwhelmed. David knew who my father was, but I didn't know if Susy had any memory of when he came to take Warren to California. And, of course, my two youngest brothers had no idea who my father was until yesterday afternoon. They probably still didn't grasp the significance of the situation. Oh to be so young and innocent! I was feeling very old and like I was carrying the weight of the world on my shoulders. I planned to talk to Mr. Steel if I could get his attention for a short time. He would help me sort through my thoughts; he was a very good listener and a very wise man!

I did find the right moment to catch Mr. Steel during the lunch hour. I told him about my brother and father showing up the day before. I told him about three years ago when my father had come to take Warren to live with him in California. I told him that I had all sorts of questions that I wanted to ask my father; I even said that I thought I might like to live with him in California.

Mr. Steel was surprised at that comment and asked how I could contemplate living with my father when I didn't even know him. I told him about how I wanted to be an actress and that I didn't think I could ever get that opportunity if I stayed on Bainbridge Island. I figured that if I lived in California, I would be closer to where the "action" was and maybe I would get my "chance." In his wisdom, Mr. Steel said, "Have a talk with your father. Ask him if you could come for a visit during the summer. Take one step at a time."

The weight on my shoulders suddenly lifted and I felt excited. I thanked Mr. Steel and went and joined my friends who were sitting in the shade of a large maple. I eagerly shared my news about the day before and about my talk with Mr. Steel. So now, the cat was out of the bag, and I was going to have to summon the courage to talk with my father. Needless to say, the rest of the afternoon at school seemed to move in slow motion. I just wanted to get home as quickly as possible and have that talk with my father.

Unfortunately, when I got home, he wasn't there. He and his friend had gone to see Century 21. I didn't let that dampen my spirits; I picked Warren's brain until he was totally exasperated. I wanted to know every detail of what life was like living with our father. Warren repeatedly told me that there was nothing special; that he had better times with our great aunt and also with Grandma and Grandpa Van Pelt. I questioned him relentlessly about them; I needed to know these people. He told me that my great aunt was very not very healthy anymore; he didn't think she would live much longer. Her name was Myra Marsh! Oh my goodness! That was the actress my mother had told me about!

That night, I watched out the window from my upper bunk. I was looking to see when my father and his friend would get back from Century 21. I knew it was late at night and that I wouldn't be able to talk with him until I got home from school the next day, but I wanted the assurance that they were actually coming back to the motel. I fell asleep without seeing them come back.

Morning surprised me; the night passed so quickly. I couldn't even remember dreaming anything. Usually I had very vivid dreams. They were filled with lots of action and amazing colors. Mom had told me it was because I was very artistic. I don't know how she knew that an artistic person would have such realistic dreams, but she was artistic and we were very much alike. Maybe she had weird dreams too. But now my dreams were not nighttime visions; they were nagging me every moment of the day! I was determined that I would go to California to pursue an acting career. I figured I would have to wait until I graduated from high school, but that was okay with me. Time was flying by so fast, I would be graduating in just a few years.

It was the last full day of school before we let out for summer vacation. As I walked by my father's apartment on the way to the bus stop, he came out and greeted me. He said that he and his friend were heading back to California. I told him that I had wanted to have a talk with him and get to know him. He said he would write and that we could get to know each other through letters. I said okay (what else could I say) and we hugged good-bye.

I continued on to the bus stop. I told Susy and David that my father was going back to California. However, I did not tell them the thoughts that were going through my mind. I was setting my course; I would write to him every week and really get to know him. I planned to go and visit him the following summer and then stay in California and somehow become an actress. I was full of childhood dreams that, at the time, I thought were very grown-up.

CHAPTER 3

A WORKING GIRL

My summer between elementary school and junior high was not the typical summer a young person, such as I, would have imagined. I was happy to help out at the motel and I certainly enjoyed meeting people from all over the country. But, like any soon-to-be-teenager, I wanted to have fun. Upmost on my agenda was spending carefree days at the beach, visiting with my friends, seeing lots of movies, reading some good books, and last, but not least, having a few good adventures.

My younger brothers and sister liked going to the beach too, so Mom found time in her busy schedule to take us to Pleasant Beach as often as possible. It was not a very sandy beach; the tide had to be out quite far before we could enjoy any soft sand. However, the best asset the beach offered was the location! Every hour a ferryboat would make its way through the Rich Passage as it traveled between Seattle and Bremerton. The waterway between Bainbridge and the mainland was quite narrow along the south end of the island. The enormous waves produced by the passing ferry gave everyone in the water a ride equal to anything found at an amusement park. We always had inner tubes with us; we knew we could count on a few minutes of rollicking fun every time the ferry went by.

Mom would often drop us off at the beach, leaving me in charge to watch my siblings. That was fine with me. They had friends with whom they would play, and it was easy to keep an eye on them when they were on the beach. They seldom wandered far from me, and on those rare occasions when they did, they came right back when I called for them.

I spent many carefree hours with my friend Kitten. We rode our bikes all over the south end of the island. There were two entrances to Fort Ward--one on the north end and the other on the south. The fort was high on a hill, so when we left on one of our many bike rides, we always had the invigorating thrill of coasting down a long, winding road. Since no energy was expended during our descent, we had plenty of steam left to pedal to our destination.

Sometimes we took the road that went past Pleasant Beach and on into Lynwood. From there, we would head west and ride along the road that hugged the water's edge out past Point White and on to Crystal Springs. When we were really feeling adventurous, we would take the north road out of Fort Ward, coast down the hill, and take a sharp right turn at the bottom onto Country Club Road. After a short distance, we would turn up a road that eventually led us to a very steep, downhill road. There was no way we could just let loose and coast down that hill! It was so steep, and the road ended abruptly at a "T." I did not have hand brakes on my bicycle, so my leg got tired from stepping back on the brake to try and slow my descent. The road was appropriately named, "Toe Jam Hill." I could picture in my mind, the countless number of people who had driven down that hill with their toes jammed onto the brake pedal of their automobiles. If they didn't break, they would cross over the "T" in the road and end up in Puget Sound!

As often as possible, I would get together with my friend Cheryl. It was difficult because we lived at opposite ends of the island. Mom was really wonderful about taking me to Seabold whenever she could. Sometimes she and my siblings would go to visit Grandma Henderson or Aunt Virginia, and I could just walk to Cheryl's from there. It was always so fun to go swimming at Cheryl's; the water was really murky, but it was warm. When we got tired of swimming, we could always take the rowboat out for a ride. I always loved to row around the little island where my friend Alice had taken me on my very first rowboat ride. Those were such happy, carefree days.

As much as I would have liked to spend my summer days drifting along in a boat or riding my bike, practicality demanded more of me. I needed to make some money. The little allowance Mom gave me for helping with the motel cleaning wouldn't buy me school clothes or give me much in the way of "fun" money. I needed to get a job. I was almost thirteen; surely I could get a job doing something. Mom came to the rescue as she always did. She spread the word and within a few days, I had my first full-time job! It was just temporary, only for one month, but I would earn five dollars a day! That meant that I would take home twenty-five dollars in one week; I would make hundred dollars in four weeks. I was really excited!

A lady, Mrs. Martin, who lived in one of Mom's new rentals needed a full-time babysitter. (Her regular sitter was an older woman who was on an extended vacation.) She was a single, working mother with four children! Her oldest daughter, Heidi, was ten, so she was quite a help, but the three younger children were a handful. Mrs. Martin and my mother decided that between Heidi and me, we could handle the three younger children. Mrs. Martin worked in Seattle, but my mother was available with the car in case of an emergency. On the first Monday in August, I went to work!

I arrived at the apartment promptly at 7:00 a.m. Mrs. Marin had to be on the 7:50 ferry. She had a list of chores for me to do in addition to tending the children. We had met the Saturday before to discuss what all of my duties would include. I could tell that she felt a little guilty about leaving me such a long list of chores. But after doing to the washing and ironing for the motel, I didn't think washing, drying, and folding children's clothing was much of a task! Preparing meals for the children wasn't a problem either; I had helped with the cooking at home for so many years, it wasn't an issue.

The big problem was potty-training! The youngest girl, Tabetha, was just learning to use her potty-chair. To be more precise, her mother wanted her to learn to use the potty-chair. Tabetha really didn't seem to be the least bit interested! Oh what a mess! It seemed that she was forever wetting her pants. Fortunately, she had lots of clothes; she went through outfit after outfit in rapid succession. I tried to just let her run around in her panties when she was inside the house, but it was August and she wanted to play outside with her brothers. Needless to say, every day was laundry day.

We tried all sorts of bribes and rewards to get Tabetha to want to use the potty. She certainly acted proud of herself when we managed to catch her at just the right moment and she succeeded in using the potty-chair. Even with my limited knowledge of child behavior, I knew that her older sister and I were the ones that were being trained and that she really wasn't ready for such an advanced skill. Tabetha was only about eighteen months old; I think her mom was just anxious to get her out of diapers.

When I arrived in the morning, the children were usually still in bed. Heidi would get up and kiss her mother good-bye and then help me prepare breakfast for the family. Just like at my house, that usually meant cold cereal. It amazed me at how many varieties of cereal were on the market! In the ten years that I could remember eating cold cereal, the choices had grown from a few to several dozen. Unfortunately, they were filled with sugar, and even I could recognize the effect a huge morning dose of sugar had on little children. Oh my goodness! No sooner was breakfast over, than they became like wild monkeys. If we had had trees in the living room, they would have been swinging from the branches. Instead, they would run around chasing each other, while screaming and laughing in uncontrollable mirth. I would chase them into their bedroom and encourage them to get dressed and brush their teeth before they went outside to play. They expended so much energy from their morning romp in the living room that by the time they went outside, they acted like normal, well-behaved children. The neighbors thought I was an amazing babysitter!

With the kids outside and their oldest sister watching them, I was able to quickly wash the breakfast dishes and get the laundry started. I fixed the beds, vacuumed, and scoured the bathroom. I would then go outside and play with the little ones while Heidi would fold the laundry and put the clothes away. She knew better than I did which clothes belonged to whom. The two boys' clothes were really difficult for me to decide; they looked the same size to me. However, Heidi knew instantly what to put into what pile and where to put them away.

Lunch was always an easy task. Whoever invented sandwiches must have become a very wealthy person. Those kids only wanted sandwiches. Peanut butter and jelly was always top on the menu. They liked tuna fish and they liked bologna, but good, old PB&J was their first choice. Milk had to have chocolate in it. Hershey's chocolate syrup came in a sixteen-ounce can. Those kids went through a couple of cans in a week! There was always a good stock kept in the upper cupboard. I suppose their mother thought they wouldn't use it up so fast if she hid it. (They all knew where the chocolate syrup was kept.) Whenever a can of chocolate got close to being empty, the three oldest children would draw straws to see who got to pour in the milk and drink straight from the can. I sometimes wondered if we were related because they loved chocolate as much as I did!

After lunch, I would put Tabetha down for a nap. I always put a diaper and plastic pants on her because I knew she would wet the bed otherwise. I wished she were potty-trained, but I hadn't come up with a brain-stormed idea as yet on how to go about it. I just put her on the potty throughout the day, hoping to catch her at the right moment. On this one particular day, I became determined to get her potty-trained!

I put her down for a nap and shooed the other children outside while I cleaned up the mess from lunch. Since the little one was sound asleep, I went outside and sat on the porch stairs, soaking up the warm afternoon sun. The boys were playing catch with a softball, and Heidi was reading a book. It definitely felt like the dog-days of summer. I was beginning to feel very drowsy, wishing I could just shut my eyes and have a nice afternoon nap. I knew I had to stay awake; I was not being paid to take a nap!

I kept fighting the urge to fall asleep. Just as I was drifting off into dream-land, I heard a cry from inside the house. Tabetha had woken up, and my laziness had come to an end. I stood up on the lower stair so quickly, I almost made myself pass out. That would have been really embarrassing! I could just picture myself falling off the stairs, flat on my face. Those boys would have laughed their heads off and Heidi would have called my mother! My mother would have driven down to the apartment filled with worry. I walked into the house thankful that I had not made a spectacle of myself.

Tabetha was in her crib, crying more loudly than usual. I entered her room and immediately smelled the most disgusting odor! Toxic fumes would have been a more appropriate description, but at that time in my life, I did not know about such things. The room wreaked! I opened the blinds and to my horror, she had poo everywhere! She was still in her crib but she had managed to smear her poo over every available object within her reach. Her diaper was lying on the sheet. She had removed it; I have no idea why. I guessed she didn't like the feel of having poo in her diaper. But why on earth did she have to smear it everywhere? Oh My Goodness! What a Mess!

I quickly went into the bathroom and started a bath running. I went outside on the porch and told the Heidi to keep an eye on the boys because I was going to be a while cleaning up the little one. I told her what her little sister had done; her eyes got as big as saucers and she said, "She has never done that before!"

Those words did not comfort me in the least. I was facing the most disgusting task I had ever faced. I remembered Mom telling me about one of my little brother's doing the same thing and how she had to methodically clean it up. I'm glad Mom had told me that story; now I was putting into practice what she had told me. I grabbed a washrag, dampened it, and went into the bedroom. I removed the rest of her clothing and washed off the majority of the poo from her body. I left the soiled rag in the crib along with all the mess and lifted her out and had her walk into the bathroom. I put her into the tub and washed her off. While I was washing her, I talked to her as though she was much older than she was.

"You made an awful mess in your crib," I told her. "Why did you do that?" I asked, as I looked directly into her eyes. "When you need to go poo, you need to go on the potty," I reminded her. "No one likes to have to clean up a big mess like you made."

She looked at me with her big, beautiful eyes and said, "Potty." I picked her up out of the tub and put her on her potty-chair. She immediately went and I praised her and she smiled. Somehow, she made a real connection with the use of the potty-chair. Right there, in that minute, she really understood what she needed, what she had done, and that she was a big girl for doing so. That was the beginning of the potty-training for real! She understood what was being asked of her and she was happy to oblige.

I put clean clothes on her and brought her outside with her sister and brothers. I asked Heidi to please watch the younger ones while I tackled the mess inside. It was a horrible job I faced, but the sooner I got to it, the quicker it would be done. I ran a bucket of water and put some pine scented cleaner in it. I really had no idea what I should use. I didn't want to call my Mom because I didn't want her to think that I couldn't handle the situation. I armed myself with several rags and went into the bedroom.

I opened the window; I wished then that I had thought to open it when I first discovered the mess. But, better late than never is what Mom always said. I pulled the bedding off of the crib mattress and carried it downstairs to the laundry room. I put it through a complete wash cycle to clean off the nasty poo before putting it through another cycle with detergent. While it was going through the first cycle, I went up and attacked that bedroom with all the gusto I could muster! I washed and rinsed, washed and rinsed. I wanted every trace of that poo gone! I wanted to be able to proudly show my employer that I had done an exceptional job of cleaning that mess up.

With everything spotless and smelling like pine, I put a fresh sheet on the mattress and a clean blanket on top. I kept the window open to air out the pine smell and went downstairs to put detergent into the washer and restart it. Back up the stairs I went to rinse out the bucket and rags and to put the rags into the dirty laundry basket for the next day. I went outside to play with the children; it was almost time to start preparing dinner!

I was exhausted; taking care of a house or large apartment and three children was a lot of work. I was so thankful that I had ten-year-old Heidi to help me. I had the kids come inside and watch the television while I prepared dinner. Again, Heidi helped me; she was such an asset to me during my time working for her mother. We set the table while the younger children washed their hands. Dinner was ready and waiting when their mom walked into the house. The first thing she said was, "I smell pine cleaner."

The proceedings of the afternoon burst forth from my mouth in an unstoppable torrent. Mrs. Martin looked at me with shock written all over her face. "None of my children have ever done that before!" My employer apologized profusely. I thanked her but reminded her that it wasn't her fault. It was really no one's fault; her daughter was just a little girl and didn't know any better. Then I told her how much headway we had made in the potty-training department. I knew that Mrs. Martin had to hear something wonderful about her children when I had just told her something bad. I think I must have said and done the right things because I got a five-dollar bonus that day!

My four-week job flew by. My mother brought us to the beach several times and even to a birthday party for a child of one of my employer's friends. Those outings put some interest into what could have become quite mundane. I soon realized what I had heard Mom and other mothers complain about. The work goes on, nothing seems to get done, no one says thank you, and I never get to talk to anyone my age! Well, it wasn't quite that bad; I had Heidi to keep me company and to share the work.

I had earned enough money to buy new clothes for school and had some left over for fun things like going to the movies. I had turned thirteen and was getting ready to enter junior high. I would get to see all of my old friends from Captain Wilkes School and be with my friends from McDonald's as well. Could life get any better than that? Actually it could. The phone rang one evening and it was for me. The boy I liked invited me to his house the next day and to stay for dinner!

CHAPTER 4

PUPPY LOVE

Warren began his relentless teasing almost as soon as I hung up the phone. "Vicki's got a boyfriend, Vicki's got a boyfriend!" He wouldn't stop; I could feel my face turning red. I wished that I had some control over what shades of red my face would turn when I blushed. Better than that, would be if I wouldn't turn red at all! Ideally, I wouldn't even get embarrassed; I would just brush off my brother's comments with a shrug of my shoulders. I wished he would stop!

I walked to my room and as I was closing the door I heard one last sing-song tease, "Vicki's got a boyfriend!" Lyrics to the song began floating through my mind. "And they called it Puppy Love, 'cause we're only in our teens." My friend, I will call him Sam, was a year older than I. He was two grades ahead of me in school and he was tall. So, it seemed like there was quite a difference in our ages. But, truth be known, he was like all boys, immature for his age! Not that I cared about his level of maturity; I liked him just the way he was. He was sweet, well-mannered, and knew lots about the outdoors.

Sam's family was renting our big house in Seabold. His mother was in real estate and loved to decorate. Mom had given her full run of the house and allowed her to decorate to her heart's content. Mom had seen it after just a couple of rooms had been redone. She had described them to me and I was very curious to see what else had been transformed. We would be moving back into the house after Century 21 came to an end; I wondered if my pink and blue room was still the same.

I spent the night tossing and turning. It seemed that every time I was facing something new in my life, I had trouble sleeping the night before. I wondered if I would ever grow out of such childish behavior. Morning finally came and I was up at the crack of dawn; no use lying in bed. My little sister was still asleep; I envied her being able to sleep so peacefully. Sometimes I wanted to talk to her at night when I couldn't sleep, but I could hear her deep breathing and knew it wouldn't be nice to awaken her. Still, I wished she were older so I could discuss my thoughts and feelings with her. Warren was impossible to talk to about anything that mattered to me, and although David was maturing rapidly, I still felt he was too young to understand what I was feeling. I couldn't find a time to use the phone for a private conversation with any of my girlfriends, so I had only myself with whom to discuss my innermost thoughts and feelings.

Mom would be taking me to Sam's house that day and then she and my younger brothers and sister would go to visit Grandma Henderson. Mom invited Warren along, saying that she could drop him off in Seabold and he could visit with his buddies. He declined the offer saying that one of his friends would be coming to pick him up. Warren asked if he could start driving the Pontiac! I gasped at the thought of Warren driving the big, old car. I loved that car, and I could only imagine Warren wrecking it. I think Mom pictured the same thing because she answered with an emphatic, "No!" He said that if he could drive the car, then he could take me to the places I wanted to go. I silently freaked inside and hoped that Mom wouldn't give in!

Around ten o'clock in the morning, we piled into the car and took off for Seabold at the other end of the island. Mom and my siblings would just have a quick visit with Grandma and then return to Fort Ward; Mom couldn't be gone from the motel for any extended length of time. I was looking forward to the day when the tourists would all go home and we could have our private lives back again. Of course, I was really looking forward to moving back to Seabold when the fair was over. I wondered if things would ever be the same again. I was older now; maybe there was no going back to those wonderful, carefree days. The boys in the Tribe were older too; life was speeding by and there was nothing we could do about it.

I was hoping that Mom would just drop me off at our big house, but that hope was in vain; I should have known better. Mom got all the kids out of the car and brought them inside when Sam answered her knock on the kitchen door. I had a warm, fuzzy feeling when I realized that Sam's family used the back kitchen door as their main entrance just like we always did. I guessed practicality won every time. Sam opened the door wide and bowed while extending his arm in a wide sweeping motion to usher us into the kitchen. He was grinning from ear to ear; he made my heart melt!

Sam's mom came into the kitchen, and she and my mother started an instant banter like two hens in a chicken coop. I don't know which of them could talk the fastest; they both were excited about the changes to our big house. Sam's mom was ready to take us on the grand tour; Sam looked at me and smiled his warm, friendly smile and I had no choice but to follow like a puppy dog. I was really curious about our house, and I decided the sooner we got the tour over, the sooner my mother and the others would leave. I wanted Sam to myself!

What a transformation! Our big, old house had gone from old and comfy to a stylish 1890's look, only brand new! Fresh wallpaper adorned the walls, bright colored paints were boldly used as accents, and even the ceilings had color! The rooms were the same sizes they had always been, but the house definitely seemed larger. It boggled my mind, that colors, patterns, and stripes (there were lots of stripes) could enlarge the look of the home's interior. Still, I hoped my pink and blue room upstairs at the south end of the hall was the same as when I had left it.

It wasn't the same and my heart was broken! I knew right then and there that Susy could have the room; it would never be the same for me again. Mom's old room downstairs was done nicely in blue flowers. There was a four-poster bed in the room which Mom said was too small for her and my dad, so I was promised the downstairs room. I was pleased and looked forward to being the only person in the house to be sleeping downstairs.

The room next to my soon-to-be room had been made into a TV room. The old sink had been removed to make more room for furniture. Mom was thrilled to have a TV room so that the kids wouldn't disturb her and her friends when they were visiting.

When the tour was over, Mom and the kids left for Grandma's house. Sam and I finally got to do whatever he had on the agenda. We really hadn't discussed that point on the phone the night before; I wondered what he had in mind. The first thing he wanted to do was take me down to my favorite tree! When he and his family had stayed at our motel before Century 21, I had told him about my favorite tree. I had given him a good description, and he knew it instantly when he saw it from up on the side porch. He found his way through the overgrown trail and decided it was his favorite tree also. With his machete, he had cleared the path and some of the undergrowth from beneath the tree. I could tell by the look of things, that he used the trail often and had made himself quite at home in my tree.

It had been a year and a half since I had climbed my tree; I could hardly wait! Sam said, "Ladies first," as he once again bowed and extended his arm in an ushering gesture toward the lowest branch. I liked the way he bowed and swept his arm. If my brothers or the Tribe members had done something so chivalrous, I would have laughed, but when Sam did it, my heart melted.

We climbed as high as we dared. I was much smaller than Sam, so I could sit up on the smaller branches. We swayed in the breeze and looked at the scenery in every direction. I couldn't help getting a lump in my throat and tears in my eyes. I was homesick for Seabold, the big house, and my tree; only two more months and my family would be moving home. After talking about our moving back to Seabold and Sam's family thinking about purchasing a home in Poulsbo, we slowly climbed down. It always saddened me to come down out of the tree; I always felt like I left a part of me high up in the branches, swaying in the wind.

We took the trail down to the beach. I shared with Sam some of the wonderful times I had had on that trail as a little child up until the time when we moved. In reality, it had only been a year and a half ago, and yet it felt like a life-time. We walked along the beach and I shared my memories of the good, old days. I even told him about skinny dipping! He laughed and said he would have liked to see that! I felt my face turn crimson and there was nothing I could do to control it; I hoped he didn't notice. If he did, he was too polite to say anything. That was one of the things I liked about Sam; he just instinctively knew how to be a gentleman.

Sam began picking up flat, round rocks to skip across the water. I helped him search for rocks but I didn't want to embarrass myself by trying to make them skip. That was a skill that I had not mastered. I could make them skip once in a while, but I was not consistent. He wanted to show me and, of course, had to put his arms around me to guide my arm and hand with his. Hmmm, I liked being taught to skip rocks! Try as he might, he soon realized that I wasn't any better with his help than without it. We laughed at my inadequacy, while I continued to find rocks and he continued to skip them.

I could have stayed on the beach the rest of the day; it was my favorite place on earth. But, we had to go back up to the house for dinner; we certainly didn't want Sam's mom to come searching for us! We were too far from the house to hear if she called for us, so we scrambled up the winding path as fast as we could go. When we reached the top of the winding section, we slowed our pace and examined the blackberry thicket as we walked by. They weren't ripe yet. I told him stories about the good, old days when Mom would make lots of blackberry pies and jam. Sam said his mom was too busy to do much of that domestic stuff; she was becoming a real estate agent.

Up at the house, we went to separate bathrooms to wash up for dinner. Sam went upstairs and I got to use the downstairs room. Our colorful mural was gone; my heart broke a little. All that time and effort my mother had spent was now covered beneath two tones of gray. The bathroom fixtures were a sandy-pink. I guess it looked alright, but I missed the old bathroom. I took care of business and went out and down the hall into the kitchen to offer assistance. Sam's mom had everything under control and just said to sit next to Sam. Sam had a younger sister and an older sister. The older sister had moved out long ago, but his younger sister was almost as young as my sister Susy! She kept giggling at me and her mom kept telling her to stop.

I can't remember what we had for dinner; I must have been too embarrassed for it to record in my memory. I liked Sam but I was definitely uncomfortable around his family. I felt like they were trying to figure out why their son liked me. I really don't know why he liked me; he never told me. In fact, after his mother drove me home, he never called me again! The puppy love ended just like that! He was in high school; I was in junior high. I think they moved to Poulsbo; I never did know. It really didn't matter to me; I had enough on my mind with going back to school and looking forward to moving home in November.

CHAPTER 5

JUNIOR HIGH

I kept looking at my reflection in the bathroom mirror. I wasn't bad-looking; I just wasn't good-looking. I was too small in all the important places and too big in the wrong places. Mom finally said I could wear a soft pink lipstick, so at least I had some color in my face. I thought that the pink on my lips made my eyes look bluer. My hair was such an insignificant color of dark blonde. I don't think the term "dishwater" was an accurate description; looking closely, I could see many different shades of blonde and brown. I even spotted a single strand that looked almost black; I yanked it out immediately!

I knew I couldn't keep hogging the bathroom. My brother Warren needed his time to get ready for school too. He was excited to be going to Bainbridge High School; it was his junior year. He had attended the ninth and tenth grades in California. He wondered if he would be ahead or behind his classmates academically. He said the school counselor/vice principal told him that he needed to take Washington State history in order to graduate. He wasn't happy about it because the other students in that class would probably be freshmen! Still he would be with most of his buddies during the school day, and he was excited.

I was excited to be with my friends. I had so many from Wilkes and now from McDonald, that I just knew school would be a blast! I wouldn't know the kids from Commodore, but they could only make up about a third of the student body. In my mind that computed to already knowing most of the kids; I could hardly wait to get to school!

Warren and I caught a much earlier school bus than David and Susy. We helped ourselves to breakfast and were out the door just as David and Susy were getting their breakfast. Poor Mom; she had to prepare breakfasts four times on a weekday morning! First Dad, then Warren and me, next David and Susy, and finally Mike and Percy. Needless to say, most of the time we subsisted on the old standby, cold cereal. As Warren and I walked to the bus stop, I couldn't stop thinking about Susy beginning the first grade. She was really excited and I would have loved to be able to see her throughout the day. I loved my little sister very much, and I knew that David would keep an eye on her; he was a good big brother.

I was eager to see the route our bus would take. Some stops I remembered from the previous year, but the route changed as we headed toward school. We stopped at places and picked up kids that I did not recognize. My eyes scanned the bus as I searched for familiar faces; there really weren't very many! The kids I did recognize looked like they were thinking the same thing I was, "who are all these people?" I comforted myself with the thought that many of them were in high school, and I really didn't need to know them.

The bus stopped at the high school to unload; the junior high kids had to walk down to our school! The junior high was at the north end of Commodore Bainbridge. The playground was on the west side of the school, so sometimes, if we were in a classroom that faced the playground, we could watch the elementary school children during their recess. Sure enough, my homeroom turned out to be one of the rooms that had windows facing the playground. I knew that we would not have recess and that the playground was off limits for kids in junior high, but sweet memories filled my mind. I wondered what this day would be like.

Our homeroom teacher walked through the door and I about fell over! He was one of Mom's tenants, and he recognized me right away. (For the sake of privacy, he will be called Mr. Wells.) We greeted each other like old friends. Really, we hardly knew each other, but he was new and so was I; it was common ground and we both were happy for it. He and his wife were expecting their first child. I naturally assumed that I would be getting some babysitting jobs; he was a neighbor to the lady I had worked for during the month of August.

I made some instant friends. Mary was one such person; she was so friendly that I just couldn't help feeling like we had known each other our whole lives. Lee, a boy I had had a crush on ever since he gave me a bracelet for Christmas at our party in the fifth grade, was also in our room. Lots of my friends from Wilkes and McDonalds were in our class. There were plenty of new kids, but if they were like Mary, I would soon get to know them.

Having a home room and changing classes for reading and math was a whole new experience for us as seventh graders. We were divided up by our ability; apparently testing in the sixth grade determined what level of math and reading we were assigned to. I guess I was an average student because I was put into the second highest math and reading classes. Many of my homeroom classmates were also in my math and reading classes. I asked my homeroom teacher about it, and he said that most kids with the same abilities were put into the same homerooms.

What was really interesting was that there were some eighth graders in our math and reading classes! I remembered some of them; they had been in my first and second grade class at Wilkes before I flunked. I would see many of my old classmates in the halls, during time set aside for changing classes or for break. I saw more of them during lunch or at intermural sports in the gym. Only a few would acknowledge that they even knew me. I had become an under-classman to them; they had no interest in a seventh grader! I saw my attackers much too often; I still got a sick feeling when I saw any of them. However, they did not seem to recognize me. I guess I had changed enough in my appearance since my first round of the second grade. More than likely, they probably had forgotten the whole episode; I wished that I could forget!

We had PE class twice a week. Boys had PE on Mondays and Wednesdays, and girls had it on Tuesdays and Thursdays. On Fridays, we got together and had dance class! I have to admit that I loved dance class. No one was allowed to be a wall-flower. We learned circle dances, square dances, and even the waltz. I still remember singing, "Oh Johnny, oh Johnny, oh!" I liked the circle and square dances the best because we got to change partners many times during a single dance. The waltz was fun when you were lucky enough to get a partner without two left feet! However, most of the boys at that age just didn't have the skill or grace to be very good dancers. There were a few exceptions!

One Friday, we were learning the waltz. I was so short that I never had a problem with being taller than my dance partner. We were asked to line up on either side of the gym; boys on one side and girls on the other. Attendance was taken while we were standing in line. Then we were told to walk forward till we met the person opposite us. I ended up with a boy who fit the bill perfectly-- tall, dark, and handsome. Well, he was only a seventh grader, but still, I considered myself very fortunate!

Our teachers asked that we spread ourselves around the gym so as not to bump into other couples. My partner and I got far away from everyone else, although we were quite close to the teachers. (Both the girls and boys PE teachers worked together to teach the dance class.) We were instructed to face each other, and the girls were to put their left hand up on our partner's right upper arm. The boys were to place their right hand on the small of their partner's back. We were to hold our free hands together. The girls got to walk backward while the boys walked forward; we were to let the boys lead us. A more accurate term would have been to "push us." "One, two, three, one, two, three," we counted out loud in unison. "Step, ball, change, step, ball, change," the chanting continued. The girls walked backwards in a large circle around the gym. The boys trudged forward, pushing their partners as though they were trying to win a race. I could hear many exclamations of, "Ouch," and "Excuse me," as we made our way around the room. I felt very lucky that my partner did not step on my toes! I had a natural inclination to dance; I was loving the moment. All of a sudden my partner said to me, "Dancing with you is like dancing with a piece of popcorn."

I looked up at him with questioning eyes, and he laughed and demonstrated. He said, "Your head bobs up and down," and then he lifted his head way up and lowered it several times while he made a sing-song noise. I couldn't help laughing, but I was very self-conscious. I felt my face turn crimson; oh how I wished I would not blush so easily! We continued waltzing until the music stopped. Then we had to applaud ourselves. I never understood if we were actually applauding ourselves or if we were applauding the music. We were listening to a record of big band music on a phonograph, so it really didn't seem like we needed to applaud that!

After lunch, we could participate in intermural games in the gym. We were required to put on our PE clothes if we were going to participate; spectators could remain in their school attire. I definitely wanted to play volleyball. There were all girl and all boy teams, plus mixed. I wanted to play both; I loved volleyball. Schedules were made up and posted on the bulletin board. We could see the day before if and who we would be playing against.

One afternoon, I had just finished playing a volleyball game. There were two games going on simultaneously. Ours had finished first, so I was walking past the other game on my way to the girls' locker room. I heard Lee call out from across the gym, "Lookout!"

I glanced his direction to see who and what we were to be on the lookout for. SMACK! I was hit dead center on my face with the volleyball! It stunned me momentarily and I stood there unable to think or move. Suddenly I gasped as I saw the blood flowing freely all over my white PE clothes! I put my hands up to my nose. One of the male teachers was to my side immediately, pinching my nose and telling me to lean my head back. He had is other arm around me as he guided me out of the gym to the girls locker room. He kicked open the door and yelled, "Man coming in!"

He walked me to the sink and said he was going to get the nurse. In the meantime, one of the female teachers had come in. She said that I needed to lean my head forward. My friends were coming in and asking if I was okay. There seemed to be an awful lot of confusion in that little area of the locker room. I just wanted to go home; I told the teacher and she asked if I was sure. "How could I not be sure," went through my mind. Sometimes grownups could be so dense!

The nurse came in by the time my nose had quit bleeding. She said that she didn't think it was broken, but it was already so swollen that she couldn't be sure. I told her I just wanted to go home and she agreed it would probably be a good idea. I changed my clothes and the female teacher soaked my white shirt and shorts in the sink filled with cold water. One of my friends went to my classroom and got my homework and brought it to the locker room. I waited in the locker room for my Mom to come and get me.

Later that day when Warren came home, he came into the house very concerned because I had not been on the bus. When he heard my story of getting hit in the face with the volleyball, he laughed like it was the funniest thing he had ever heard. I never understood his sense of humor.

Even though I was now again with girls whom I had been in Girl Scouts with from Wilkes, I continued to meet with our troop on the south end of the Island. I knew we would be moving back to Seabold before long, but I would just have to cross that bridge when I came to it. I had more than enough to think about!

Friday and Saturday nights were always a big deal for kids on Bainbridge Island. Most of us went to see the movie at the theater in Lynwood. There was only one theater and sometimes we didn't really care what was playing. The important thing was to meet up with our friends and have a good time. One Friday night, on October 12th, 1962 was such a night.

CHAPTER 6

A STORM TO REMEMBER

School had been back in session for about a month. I had made many new friends, several of whom were boys. During music class on Friday, October 12, a few of us decided to meet later that evening at the Lynwood Theater. I knew that my older brother Warren and my younger brother David would probably be going also, but we never sat together. It was an unspoken rule in our house to sit with your friends, not your siblings!

When the bell rang for school to be over, the music class, which met in the annex at the high school, left in boisterous laughter and good cheer. It was a Friday afternoon, the sun was shining, and a lot of us would be getting together in a few hours to have some more fun. Had we been listening to the news or a weather report we may have changed our plans, but as it was, our thoughts were on watching a movie, eating candy, drinking sodas, and yes, dare I say, holding hands!

I noticed during the bus ride home that the weather went from October sunshine to October dreary in record time. Still, all looked calm on the home front, and none of us had any reason to think otherwise. We never bothered to turn on the television when we got home.

I just wanted to hurry and finish my homework so that I wouldn't have that nagging feeling over the weekend. I had no idea what my brothers were doing. I closed the door to my bedroom, climbed up to the top bunk, and began doing math problems. I liked math; I was good at it. Of course, I wasn't very good at story problems; most of the time it took me forever to understand what was being said. I thought it rather strange since I loved to read! I had lots of reading, U.S. history, and science. I still had eat supper too; life can sure be hectic when you're in junior high!

Mom called us for dinner around 6pm. We always waited to eat until Dad got home from work. He worked in Seattle for the school district as a maintenance worker. I believe he mostly did gardening-type jobs, but I never knew and never asked. What I did know was that he was a good father and a good step-dad to Warren and me. He would happily take us to the movie and pick us up when it was over. He never complained about taking us anywhere; we were very fortunate.

The family that owned the theater lived in Seabold. We were friends with them. We didn't get any special treatment because of that relationship, but it was nice to know that if there were a problem of any kind, we could trust this man and woman to take good care of us. I'm sure most of the parents on Bainbridge felt that way; leaving their kids at the movie was a safe thing to do.

We left for the movie around 6:30 pm. We liked to get to the movie early enough to meet up with our friends and find a good seat before the lights were turned off. We also liked to buy our treats before the movie began so we wouldn't miss any of the action. Sometimes we would miss previews of upcoming movies or part of the cartoon because the lines were so long at the concession. That family worked fast and furious to take care of all those kids wanting to spend their money; and they were always smiling!

No one said anything about the weather; it was not a topic of discussion among young people my age. We chatted about school and choir, about so and so's hairdo or haircut, and about what teachers we liked and disliked. I was sitting next to Johnny, the current boy I liked. I think he liked me too. He hadn't said so, but he had phoned me at home a few times and taken hold of my hand when we sat down in the theater! The lights dimmed and the previews of upcoming movies started. A couple of the girls sitting at the end of our row were still chattering quietly. Someone from behind us told them to "Shut up!"

We held hands in the dark. It really wasn't romantic, or anything close to it. He was holding my right hand in his left and his right hand was busy pushing popcorn into his mouth. He had the bag of corn on his lap. He kept offering me popcorn and I kept declining. I just wanted to hold his hand; if I let go to eat some popcorn, he may not hold it again. For one thing, it would be all buttery and the thought of holding greasy hands did not make a pleasant picture!

The movie had just begun when we were suddenly shrouded in blackness! There was a loud gasp as though the entire audience had inhaled in unison; then silence! No one moved a muscle, you could have heard a pin drop. It was so black, we could not see the people sitting next to us. Kids began to whisper and I could hear a few younger children starting to cry. I don't think any of us had ever been at the theater when the electricity went out. It was scary!

The owner of the theater stood up at the doorway to the concession. He had a flashlight and he told us all to remain in our seats and to keep our voices to a whisper. He said that we were having a wind storm and that the power had gone out. He informed us that as our parents arrived to pick us up, he would call our names, and we could then leave. He didn't want anyone going outside until their parents came.

His rules seemed sensible to my friends and me; we could just continue to sit where we were and quietly talk and still have a great Friday night out! That's just what we were doing when suddenly, Johnny's mom came into the theater screaming, "Johnny, where are you? We're having a hurricane!"

Bedlam broke loose; everyone was up out of their seat in a flash! No one was whispering any longer. Johnny had slumped down in his seat, totally embarrassed by his mother. She had a flashlight and was frantically walking down the aisle, shining the light into the faces of teenagers, looking for her son. Before she even got to us, Johnny stood up and said he needed to leave. Away he went with his mom; the rest of us sat back down in the dark, whispering and waiting. We waited quite a while.

Parents finally began arriving and since order had been restored, the theater slowly, yet systematically relinquished its patrons. It was a very unusual night; kids were actually glad to see their parents come to pick them up before the movie was scheduled to be over! However, my brothers and I were not so fortunate. My dad didn't come for a long time. The theater owner had tried to phone him but the line was dead. He didn't want to take us home for fear of passing my dad or missing him somewhere along the way. I felt bad; I told him to go ahead and take his family home, that we would be okay. He and his wife had two vehicles at the theater. She took their girls and left for Seabold; he said he would stay until my dad showed up.

Since we were the last kids waiting for a ride, the owner had locked up the theater. There was a sheltered area where the ticket booth was, and he said we could sit in there. My brother Warren had a friend with him. He was wearing a trench coat. He unbuttoned it and held it open as he leaned into the wind. The wind filled the coat like a parachute and the boy simply laid down toward the wind. He didn't fall to the ground; he actually laid in a forty-five degree angle. I had never seen anything like that before. Warren was so excited and wanted to borrow his trench coat so he could try too. Warren couldn't do it as well as his friend. I think because he was shorter, the wind didn't catch the coat in quite the same way. Still, they were having fun. The moon kept peeking between the sailing clouds, so it was easy to see what was going on. It wasn't raining; the wind was just blowing harder than I had ever known.

The reason my dad was so long in getting to us was that a tree had fallen across the winding road leading down from Fort Ward. He had to turn around in the dark on that narrow, winding road and go back home and get a chain saw. Then he had to saw the tree in a couple of places to remove it from the road. The poor man was visibly tired and much stressed! He shook hands with the owner of the theater and we piled into the car.

That was a very scary ride home! The wind was shaking the car. Dad was having to swerve to miss flying branches and debris. Power poles were down and lines were all over the road! Luckily there were no trees across the road until we reached the winding hill. Dad had to drive very slowly, so he could see ahead and around the curves before he got into them. A tree suddenly crashed onto the road in front of us! He quickly turned toward the right and applied the brakes. Since he had been driving so slowly, we had no problem. He and Warren and my brother's friend climbed out of the car and quickly got to work to remove that tree from the road. I was so scared; I didn't know what to do. I just kept silently praying that we would be alright and that all our friends got home safely.

The ride home took about forty minutes; it was normally a ten min-ute ride at the most. The lights were out at home too. Mom had some candles burning and a kerosene lantern lit in the family/dining room. The wind was blowing so hard, she was afraid to have Warren, Susy, and I sleep in our end of the apartment. There were some very tall fir trees across the driveway that circled the motel. If we stayed out in the family/dining room, she would feel better. I wasn't about to argue with Mom on that one! I grabbed a candle, and Warren and his friend and I went into our end of the apartment and retrieved our things for the night.

Back into the family room we went, trying to not listen too closely to the sound of branches hitting the roof. We had one sofa in the

family room. That's all there was room for because of the large dining room table that took up most of the space. I got the sofa and the
two older boys got the floor. David shared a room with my younger
brothers, and Susy was on the other end of the sofa. We tried to settle
down for some sleep.

Just when I thought, I might possibly drift off in spite of the
loud wind, the front door suddenly blew open! The wind blew full
force right into the family room; magazines and anything else made
of paper went flying in all directions. Warren and I arrived at the
door together and managed to close it. I know that I could not have
shut it without his help; the wind was really strong! Mom came out
into the room to assess the damage. She really couldn't see much
because the only light was from the moon outside. She gave her
usual exclamation of, "Oh My God," and went back into her room
and shut the door. My little sister was sound asleep on the other end
of the sofa. I wondered in awe how she could sleep through something like that storm!

The next morning was a Saturday, so at least we didn't need to
get ready for school, and Dad didn't need to go to work. We had very
few guests by then; the fair was going to be over in about a week. The
electricity was off in all the apartments, and we had no phone service.
Mom did not try to encourage any of her guests to stay on. She said
that she would refund their money if they left early; what else could
she do? At least the sun was shining!

CHAPTER 7

OLD CIDER

We were very fortunate to have nice weather following the Big Blow. We had no electricity for a week, and school did not get back in session until the following Wednesday; only about half the students came back the day the schools reopened. So many homes were without power; it was probably difficult to get ready for school, if residents knew about it at all.

We enjoyed some nice autumn weather and plans were being made to move back to our big house in Seabold. We planned to move back over the Thanksgiving weekend. Dad would have the extra time needed to make the move, and we would be home from school. David and Susy would have to change schools, but I wasn't in the least bothered because I attended the only junior high on the island. My brother was in the only high school. I could hardly wait until the Thanksgiving weekend. However, we still had Halloween to get through, plus about four more weeks of school before the move. Time moved so slowly when I was in a hurry.

Warren had been pestering Mom to let him drive the Pontiac. His reasoning was that the old car just sat there, and it would be beneficial for the engine to be used on a regular basis, rather than sitting for prolonged periods of time. He said that the engine would freeze up, and then no one would ever be able to drive it again. I guess Warren finally made a good argument because the next thing I knew, Warren was given permission to drive the old car.

I remember watching him that first afternoon. He had gone to drive it out of the carport where it was parked and bring it to the front of our apartments. Then he had to sit there with the motor running and try all the switches while Mom walked around the outside of the car, making sure all the lights were working. Warren had to show Mom that he knew how to use the proper hand signals. He was annoyed with Mom and I was annoyed with him. I felt sure that he was going to wreck the old Pontiac, and my heart was breaking before it had even happened. (I always did have an overactive imagination.)

Halloween was going to be on a Wednesday that year, so the weekend before was when most kids would be attending any scheduled Halloween parties. I wasn't going to a party; I really had very little interest in Halloween since I felt like I was too old to go trick-or-treating anymore. Warren was going to his friend's house in Seabold. He said that it wasn't a party, just a get-together with some of his buddies. He asked if he could take the Pontiac!

I instantly had a sinking feeling in the pit of my stomach; I knew letting him take the car was a bad idea. I hoped that Mom would feel what I was feeling. Instead, she said that would be fine, as long as he was careful and didn't speed. He promised he would be good and he was very excited. He had no idea what time he would come home, but Mom didn't seem to mind. It was still daylight on Saturday afternoon when he left Fort Ward for Seabold. He was so excited; I was filled with foreboding. I had never noticed how short Warren was until he sat behind the steering wheel of the Pontiac. It was such a big, old car, and he suddenly looked very young and inexperienced.

Saturday evening was like any other Saturday night. We had gone to the movies the night before, so we stayed home and watched TV.

I stayed up late, at least until 11:30 p.m., and Warren had not come home yet. I really didn't expect him to be home that early; I was just hoping. Everyone else had gone to bed; I shut off the TV, turned off the lights, and fumbled my way into my bedroom. I don't know why I always worried about waking my little sister; she slept like a log! I climbed up onto my bunk and said a prayer, especially for Warren's safe return. I crawled under the covers and lay awake for quite a while, hoping to hear when he came home.

Sometime in the middle of the night, I awoke to hear him come into the house. I heard him running water in the bathroom and when he shut his bedroom door. I heard nothing else after that and fell back asleep.

Early the next morning, before the sun was up, I was rudely awakened to the most retching sound! Warren was heaving his insides out in the bathroom, adjacent to my bedroom. I had never heard anyone be so sick in all my life; it was awful! He would heave and howl then heave some more. I could tell that his stomach was empty but the heaves kept coming. I climbed out of my bunk and went to wake up Mom. Our family utilized two apartments which were connected by a make-shift hallway through a large storage unit. Any noise coming from our end of the apartment certainly could not be heard in the other end of the adjoining apartment. Mom needed to know what was happening to Warren!

I knocked on her bedroom door and she immediately answered. I informed her that Warren was really sick and she better come. She was up and out of her room in a flash. Even my dad got up; he really was a concerned parent. They followed me into our end of the apartment and stood outside the bathroom door listening to the horrid sounds. When the first lull in the retching occurred, Mom knocked on the door and asked Warren if he was alright. I could hear the tears in his voice when he answered and said he was okay.

Mom responded that she doubted he was okay and that he better unlock the door. He said he didn't want to, that he would be alright. My dad then spoke up and said that Warren better open the door immediately, or he would go and get a screwdriver and open the door himself! Now things were getting very interesting!

Warren was obviously over the worst of his illness; he kept making moaning sounds, but at least he wasn't retching. Mom coaxed a little more and Warren finally opened the door. A horrid smell drifted out of the bathroom and filled our end of the apartment. I hurried and ran to the living room door and flung it wide open! The fresh smell of clean, autumn air flowed into the room and helped to curb the repugnant odor that had enveloped our living space. Warren's bedroom and our bathroom were a mess!

Mom asked if he had eaten something that had gone bad or if he had drunk something to have caused his terrible illness. Warren then told us the story of the cider.

The year before, when Warren was still living in California, his buddies attended the annual cider squeeze at the Seabold Community Hall. They helped out just like they did every year and then they brought some cider home. That time, however, because they were teenagers, they had the bright idea to let some of the jugs sit for a year and then open them for the Halloween party that they planned to hold. They were really happy that Warren had come home because that meant all of them could have the fun of drinking fermented apple cider.

Warren said that it didn't taste good, but since his friends were drinking it, he decided he would too. (I always knew that boys were not the brightest of creatures!) Each of those boys had consumed about a gallon of the foul liquid! Mom told Warren that he would have to clean up his room and the bathroom; that seemed like punishment enough. She phoned one of his friend's mother to see if her son had gotten ill also. Yes, he had and so had their other friends. No one went to the doctor and they all survived. We never knew if they had food poisoning or some kind of bad reaction to alcohol. Warren vowed that he would never drink an alcoholic beverage again; I believe that he never did.

CHAPTER 8

HOME, SWEET HOME

U ndoubtedly, the best day of my life was the day we moved back to our big house in Seabold. Century 21 and the Parkview Apartments were now ancient history! Even though I had some awful memories of things that had happened during my early childhood, the good far outweighed the bad. I was so happy to be home; I felt as if I would burst!

There was so much to do to get resettled in our old home. Bedrooms were assigned and I was given the one downstairs, next to the television room. Susy got my old room, David was in his old room, the younger boys were in the old playroom, and Warren got his old room. Mom and Dad were upstairs where Mom had been accosted by the bat when I was five years old. I still remembered that night as though it had happened the night before. The worst memory of their room was the night I dreamed that Captain Hook was making me walk the plank. Those memories were enough to make me grateful to have the room downstairs!

The blue room, as we called it, had been initially decorated by my mother. The tenant had done a few things to make it more comfortable.

It was a beautiful room; the wallpaper matched the bedspread, which was covered in a rose pattern consisting of various shades of blue. The canopy also had a matching cover, as well as the fabric skirt around the built-in vanity. The bed was double, so if I had any girlfriends over for the night, we would probably end up sleeping together. I hadn't figured out how that arrangement would work, but I didn't dwell on the thought. Blue was one of my favorite colors; the room was perfect!

There were phone calls to make; I had to call my best friends and let them know I was back. Of course, Cheryl was at the top of the list, but my cousin Judy was next in line. Judy was older than me and two years ahead in school, but we got along really well. Her brother Kenny was in my grade. Paul, their little brother was a couple years younger; I never did know how old he was. They lived close-by and I was looking forward to lots of fun times with them.

I didn't call the Tribe next door. My sister Susy and their little sisters were playmates. I figured between Susy and my brother David, the boys in the Tribe would know we were back in record time. I was looking forward to some fun times with them again. Unfortunately, I was older and had lots of homework, Girl Scouts, and church activities, so playing with the Tribe boys became a thing of the past. Time spent with my girlfriends was much more important than playing ball! We found it more enjoyable to talk about boys than to actually be with them!

Mom still owned the Parkview Apartments and had renters in all the units. She had also bought two, big old, Victorian-style buildings in Fort Ward. One of the buildings was a duplex; the other consisted of four units. My month-long babysitting job had taken place in one of the four units, and my homeroom teacher lived in one of them. I didn't know who lived in the other units. Dad was working in Seattle, and with mom having so much to do, I felt the responsibility to help out at home as much as possible. Life was very complicated!

Girl Scouts was just as fun as ever. We were older now and had very stylish uniforms. They consisted of a dark-green A-line skirt, a white blouse, and our badge banner. We also wore a beret and even white gloves when the occasion called for it. I felt very classy when I put on my uniform. We still met at the same house we met at before we had moved to Fort Ward. I was so happy that all of us were still together. Our leader was amazing and we all appreciated her very much.

Our Girl Scout leader and her family, which included one of my classmates, did have a very unhappy experience that year. One day, their son was outside playing on their rope swing, and he didn't come inside when he was called. That was unusual because he was normally an obedient son. He was found hanging from the tree, dead. Somehow, it must have bounced when he was playing and got caught around his neck. It was truly the most devastating experience any of us young people had ever known. Our friends just didn't die; we were too young and full of life for that to happen!

We didn't meet at our friend's house for Girl Scouts for a couple of months after that. Our classmate was absent from school for only about a week. On the day she came back, it got to be too much for her. We were in the same reading class, and she sat across the aisle from me. She had opened her desk top and was hiding under it, silently crying so no one would see her. I got up from my seat and walked up to the teacher's desk and whispered to her what the problem was. I thought that the teacher may let her be excused to the restroom. WRONG! She said to ignore her and it would pass!

Of all the cruel and unfeeling things for a teacher to say! That teacher was full of them. I sometimes wondered why she had become a teacher; she obviously did not like kids! Some of the other kids in our class had noticed that she was crying, and we were all trying to hold back our tears of sympathy. (Nowadays, students and teachers talk about their feelings of fear or grief. No one is expected to suffer alone and in silence.)

It was a welcome day when we went back to Girl Scouts at our friend's house, but we all felt a little awkward and didn't know what to say or how to express our sympathy. We didn't want to arouse sad feelings, but we wanted that whole family to know that we cared very deeply. It was our leader who led the way; she hugged and comforted us! I not only learned about scouting from our leader, I learned about compassion, understanding, and inner strength. What a remarkable woman!

Being back in Seabold meant attending the Methodist Church. I was elated to once again be able to walk across the street and through the woods to the road that led to the church. The trail was still well-worn, and since I was older, it seemed to not be as long. Often, I would meet my friend Cheryl up on the road as I emerged from the woods, and we would walk together to church. It was wonderful to mingle with my extended family and friends on Sunday mornings. I always felt bad that my immediate family had no inclination to join me.

I was very impressionable and believed everything our minister said; I had no reason to doubt him. He had always spoken the truth, as far as I knew. I loved the Bible stories, and I wanted to grow up to be a really good Christian woman. I looked at the minister's wife and thought her to be a prime example and role model. The minister and his wife were very different from my parents; I loved my parents, but I knew I wanted something more.

I became really involved in the youth activities at the church. In November our congregation voted to move and remodel our church! I had never conceived of such a notion; I couldn't imagine our wonderful, old church being moved to a new location, getting an addition, and being remodeled. All the wonderful memories of that church were going to be forgotten; how could they let this happen? Here I was, happy to be back in my home, sweet home, and now my church was going to move!

CHAPTER 9

SMOKING

It seemed that smoking cigarettes was the "cool" thing to do. My oldest brother had smoked ever since I was old enough to observe the world around me. My mother smoked every chance she got. My dad rarely smoked; he said he really didn't like it. However, lots of my friends were taking a few puffs to see if they enjoyed it. I had memories of my early childhood trips to the hospital because of asthma and pneumonia. I really was afraid that smoking might trigger the onset of one or the other, but at my age, peer pressure was master of the universe.

My cousin wanted to try smoking and asked me to join her; I was spending Friday night at her house. I had no idea where she got the cigarettes from; I could not recall ever having ever seen her mother smoke. I thought her dad did, but I really couldn't remember having seen him either. I didn't ask and she didn't tell! We went outside, far from the house, and lit up. She gave me instructions on how to put the end of the cigarette into my mouth, suck in while holding the lighter to the other end, and when I noticed it beginning to glow, it was ready to smoke. Maybe it was ready for her to smoke, but choke was a more accurate description of what I was attempting to do. I realized immediately that I had better not inhale; I wasn't getting asthma, but my ears were plugging up and I was feeling a little nauseated. Those were sure signs of an allergy. I didn't want her to think I was a sissy, so I pretended to be enjoying the whole ordeal, but I secretly vowed that I would never smoke again!

When we had taken the last puffs from the cigarettes, we threw the butts on the ground and stomped them out. Then we each took a stick of chewing gum, popped it into our mouth, and thought we were very clever. We walked back to the house, went inside and up to her room without her mother giving us the slightest bit of attention. We thought we were so smart; we never did get caught!

On the following Monday our seventh-grade art class was given an assignment. We were instructed on how to make a collage and provided with lots of old magazines to cut out pictures. I didn't waste one second in deciding the theme of my work of art. "Smoking more but enjoying it less." That was a phrase used in a popular cigarette advertisement. Apparently, one particular brand of cigarette gave the smoker more enjoyment than the other brands; frankly, I doubted it! But, I knew exactly what my artwork would depict. I would show a scowling man with his mouth full of many different brands of cigarettes. The entire background of the collage would consist of as many packages of cigarettes as I could find pictures for. I knew I was creating a meaningful work of art.

Upon completion of our masterpieces, they were put on display along the walls of the hallway. Not only did I receive an "A" for my project, the Winslow Fire Department asked if they could have the collage to put up on a wall in the fire station. That was fine with me; no one had ever made such a fuss over any of my artwork prior to that. (Thirty years later, my masterpiece still adorned their wall.)

My vow to never smoke again did not last long; I was a succor for peer pressure. Only a few months later I was spending the night at a friend's house, and she had a package of cigarettes. She wanted to smoke them and wanted me to join in the fun. I told her that I really didn't like to smoke, but she said to not inhale; I guess she didn't want to smoke alone. Her mom was gone and we had the house to ourselves. We sat right in the living room, not trying to hide ourselves in the least! I asked if she were worried about her mom coming home and catching us, but she said that her mom wouldn't care! She said that her mom thought if we wanted to smoke, it was our own business.

I couldn't imagine any mother being that carefree! However, at the moment, I was pleased that she was so that we did not have to go outside on a chilly night. There were definitely some advantages of having a carefree mother!

True to her word, we smoked the entire package of cigarettes. I did not inhale once and I did not get asthma. I did, however, get a horrible headache in addition to the nausea and plugged up ears. I was practically deaf until the next day! My head felt like it was going to explode; I had to take aspirin twice during the night.

The next morning, I again vowed that I would never smoke another cigarette and I never did!

CHAPTER 10

THE CHRISTMAS PARKA

Christmas in 1962 was very different for me. I was now thirteen and a mature young woman, at least I thought so. There were no toys on my wish list, only clothes. It wasn't that I really needed clothes; I just wanted new clothes so that I would feel like I looked good. I knew lots of other girls would be getting new clothes for Christmas, and I wanted to be just like everyone else. Peer pressure probably wasn't as bad as my imagination; mine was definitely overactive and I continually thought the worst. I thought my clothes were dowdy compared to those of the girls I considered to be popular.

It was no use trying to explain my feelings to my mother; she simply didn't understand or refused to. We did not have a lot of money and there were six children still living at home. New clothes were expensive and my younger siblings needed clothes too, and so I resigned myself to something reasonably new from one of the local rummage sales. I always hoped that no one would recognize their discarded skirt, blouse, or dress. I was always nervous when I first wore a rummage sale item to school. I figured everyone would be staring at me and thinking, or worse yet, saying, "Oh look, Vicki is wearing my old outfit."

School let out for vacation on Friday, December 21; it really was very close to Christmas. It seemed like we usually had a few more days of vacation before the actual holiday was upon us. Not so that year; we were in school as long as possible. The bus ride home was exceptionally fun because everyone was filled with anticipation. I guess kids in junior high and high school thought more about the materialistic side of Christmas instead of the true reason for the season which was the birth of Christ.

In my mind they were like two separate occasions. The religious side of Christmas was the birth of Christ and all the traditions that went along with the celebration such as church pageants, the story from the Book of Luke, Christmas carols of a sacred nature, nativity sets, and the star on top of the Christmas tree. The fun side of Christmas was decorating the house, eating lots of good food, visiting friends and family, singing the fun songs of Christmas, and getting presents. I knew many people only celebrated the fun side of Christmas. I liked that I celebrated both sides; it made the holiday twice as fun!

On Saturday, we went with Dad to my cousin's house to cut down a Christmas tree. They had lots of young fir trees growing in their field. There were many to choose from; it was not an easy choice. We were going to set the tree up in the corner of the living room, next to the big double doors that separated the living and dining rooms. That meant that the tree would be half hidden from view. We wanted a tree that would not stick out too far in the front because the foot traffic passing by the tree was often very busy. The tree could not be too tall because the tree topper was at least a foot by itself. We also wanted the branches to be evenly spaced so as not to have any bare spots. Only David, Susy, and I accompanied Dad on the Christmas tree expedition; that meant four differing opinions had to merge and become united in our selection. Finally, out of sheer freezing desperation, we settled on our tree and Dad sawed it down; like it or not, we had to live with it!

We all helped Dad drag the tree to the car. He had an old blanket that he put on top of the car, and then he laid the tree on top of the blanket. He tied some cord around the tree by passing the cord through the slightly opened windows of the car; thankfully, we had only a short drive to get home. We piled into the car, anxious to get home and begin the fun of decorating. I loved to decorate; transforming the appearance of anything was a task I thoroughly enjoyed. I guess that's partly why I wanted to be an actress when I grew up; I would be able to transform myself into someone else. However, at that time in my life, I had to settle on decorating the house for Christmas.

Sunday church service was nice, but I missed the wonderful pageants we had had when I was a young child. It seemed like the older I got, the more busy people became; they had less time to devote to the old traditions. I loved looking at the beautiful decorations at the church and the tree, of course, but it was not the same as I remembered. The early years of the Seabold Community Church were etched in my heart and mind forever.

Monday was Christmas Eve and we were excited. We would be going to Grandma Henderson's for dinner. The extended family had grown so much that the gift exchange had become less of an event. Only the small children were getting gifts; each family was doing their own gift exchange at home. It didn't matter to me; the best thing about dinner at Grandma's was the food. Everyone who wanted to bring something did; the feast presented had never been better! I was not a picky eater by the time I was thirteen, and I didn't care about watching my weight. I was small and I could eat as much as I wanted and not gain an ounce. I considered myself very fortunate!

As old as I was, I still enjoyed hanging a stocking for Santa to fill. My brother Warren wanted nothing to do with the old tradition. Mom tried to coax him but he was adamant; he would not participate! The rest of us children did not hesitate in the least; our stockings were hung up and we wanted to go to bed so that Santa could come.

Mom and I stayed up and watched, *It's a Wonderful Life,* and then she tried to shoo me off to bed. I told her that I wanted to help fill the stockings. She said that I could put some oranges, apples, and nuts into the stockings but that Santa would have to do the rest. I had fun playing the part of an elf and finally went to bed feeling like a grownup. I could hear Mom scurrying around the house; I wanted to open my door a crack and try to spy. Unfortunately, my door only faced the hallway, so I wouldn't be able to see into the living room where all the action was.

I threw back the covers, laid down, and pulled the covers tight around me; I always slept better if I felt like a bug in a rug. I think I was always a little afraid of the boogie-man my older brothers had taunted me about when I was a little girl. Christmas Eve was no different; I needed the covers snug around me in order to fall asleep.

I awoke in the morning to the squeals and laughter of my little brothers. Susy and David were quietly waiting for the rest of the household to be awoken from our boisterous siblings. Mom came downstairs and went directly to the kitchen to start the coffee. Dad came downstairs a few moments later, fully clothed and ready for the day. He was in a very good mood; he always kept his good nature tuned very low. If he had been a radio or television, the volume would have been set very quiet; that was just the way he was.

Warren said that he wasn't coming down for the festivities but Mom insisted. She had gifts for him and I could tell that he was pleased. I could not understand why he didn't want to participate in our family activities; he was as much a part of the family as I was. David was given gift duty and passed out gifts to all of us. As soon as all the packages were delivered, my siblings started tearing paper and ribbons! I always like to keep my paper and ribbons nice; I thought they could be used again.

I honestly can't remember what anyone else got for Christmas that year. The two gifts that I received made such an impression on me that all else was crowded out. I got a new dress! It was a size Junior

Petite 5. I had never heard of a size like that before. Mom was anxious for me to try it on because she had guessed at the size when looking in the store. It was a perfect fit. Mom was as pleased as I was. She said it was always so difficult to shop for me because she never knew what size I was. She knew that from then on she could find me clothes in the Junior Petite Department.

The last box I opened took my breath away. It was a black, furry jacket with a hood trimmed in sheep's wool. It had the trim around the bottom edge also. On the back was a colored totem pole design. The inside was made from a bright, red, quilted fabric. The jacket was reversible. Mom said it was called a Parka. I loved it; it was the prettiest jacket I had ever had. Mom whispered to me that it cost $49.95 and to never let Dad know; he would be upset for her spending so much money. I promised I would never tell and I never did.

Mom said that my Parka would be warmer if I wore the furry side on the inside with the red, quilted fabric facing out. However, when I tried it on that way, I felt like I was too confined. The fur made me feel like I was stuffed into something too small. I liked the fur on the outside; I could move freely and it felt very warm to me.

(I didn't know it at the time, but I would wear that parka for the next forty-one years. I never outgrew it and it never seemed to go out of style. I wore it all the years I was raising my children, even through my pregnancies. I finally gave it to a charity when the sheep's wool started to thin. My mother passed away years before I quit wearing the parka; she was so pleased that I wore it for so long.)

CHAPTER 11

STOLEN KISS

Living next door to a family of boys can have many advantages. The most obvious is a never ending source of amusement. Perhaps a better description would be recreation. I'm really not sure how to describe it; rest assured it was never boring!

I had played with most of those boys since I was four years old; they were sort of like brothers to me. In fact, because of our closeness in age, I felt much more akin to them than to my own brothers. During my tomboy years, they had been the best playmates a girl like me could have. When I wanted to participate in activities preferred by the male of our species, there was always at least one Tribe member ready and willing.

One of my favorite pastimes was taking a wild ride down their cable from the cherry tree to the pear tree. There was a pulley attached to the cable and a short rope attached to the pulley. A piece of wood was secured to the rope for a seat. A thin cord was attached to the bottom of the seat to pull the contraption up to the branch in the tree where we began our descent. We would grab the cord and hang onto it while we either climbed the hill to the base of the cherry tree or climbed higher up into the tree to start from where the cable was attached. We would then pull the cord hand over hand until we could grab onto the rope. Then we would swing our legs onto the seat, straddling the rope, and speed down the cable. The distance down the hill to the pear tree must have been a hundred feet or more. There was an old mattress leaning up against the trunk of the pear tree to crash into if we didn't slow enough during our descent. The pulley and cable were the equivalent of an amusement park ride; we loved it!

Unfortunately, we have to grow up. I was no longer a child when our family moved back to the big house in Seabold; I was a teenager. I really didn't look like a teenager, and I was only in the seventh grade, but I was getting to be too old to act like a boy. Although there were plenty of opportunities to act like a girl, I wanted to be a tomboy when I was with my Tribe buddies. The fact that I had become a teen-ager really put a damper on things!

One Saturday I had been over at the Tribe's house, just hang-ing around with my friends. I don't remember what activity we had been engaged in, but we always had a good time. I mentioned that I had better get home to help Mom get dinner ready, and I headed across the field toward our house. I hadn't gone very far when the oldest Tribe boy caught up to me. He asked, "Can I walk you home?"

I was quite taken aback by the question! Not once could I remem-ber any of those boys ever asking to walk me home! Instantly all sorts of thoughts came flooding into my mind. "Why does he want to walk me home? Did his brothers put him up to it? Does he like me?"

"I guess so," was all that managed to come out of my mouth. I was already worrying about what may happen when we reached my house. Would he just say good-bye and turn around and walk home? Would my brother Warren see us and start his relentless teasing? Would David see us and tell Mom? These thoughts were going through my mind when he said, "Can I hold your hand?"

Now I was really in a panic state; he was serious! I had never thought of him or any of the Tribe members as boyfriends; they were just friends who happened to be boys! I didn't want to hurt his feelings and I really could see no harm, so I innocently said, "Okay."

I was very inexperienced about boys as boys, versus boys as friends. I could hang around and play with guys all day long and have so much fun. I liked some boys at school as boys, and I had had my boyfriend who used to live in our big house, but I had never held hands with any of them! Here I was, holding hands, walking beside someone who I thought was just a friend. He seemed to have suddenly thought of me as a girl instead of just a friend. This was indeed a dilemma; I was not ready for this at all!

When we reached the fence at the edge of the field, he lifted the third barbed wire and pushed down on the second wire so I could easily climb through. As I started to bend over and lift my leg, he suddenly let go of the wires and put his hands on my shoulders. I stood up to face him and ask what he was doing. He had the strangest look on his face, and his voice sounded like he might break out in tears at any moment. He said, "Aren't you going to kiss me good-bye?"

Horror of horrors! What was he thinking! I did not want to kiss him good-bye or hello or any other kind of a kiss! I had never kissed a boy and I didn't want to start then! I had had my eye on a boy at school that I thought I might like to kiss, but kissing my neighbor just wasn't anything I had ever planned on! I didn't know how to get out of the situation without hurting his feelings. I had never talked to Mom about a situation like I was facing; I had never talked with my girlfriends about such a predicament.

I had always thought I needed to make people happy and do whatever I could to keep the peace. This time was no different. Swallowing my fear, I said, "Okay." I lifted my face and he bent over and we kissed. I didn't know how to kiss and I don't think he did either because I didn't think it was anything spectacular. In fact, I just wanted out of there as fast as I could scurry! I didn't let my lips linger on his; I pulled away quickly, separated the wires on the fence, and climbed through as fast as I could. I ran to our house, yelling a quick good-bye, scampered up the steps, and threw open the door in one breath.

I let myself into the house, shut the door, and leaned against it, hoping that he did not feel inclined to follow me home. My heart was pounding in my ears, and I was sure I was going to be sick! I walked down the hall toward the kitchen and saw my brother Warren seated on the sofa in the dining room.

I didn't want the Tribe boy to think I liked him as a boy, so I thought maybe Warren could be of assistance to me. I told Warren what happened. BIG MISTAKE! He doubled over with his arms wrapped around his stomach and responded with, "Who would want to kiss you? Yuck!"

I tried to get Warren to understand that I wanted his assistance in talking to the Tribe boy and to let him know that I didn't want him for a boyfriend. I wanted him to gently explain that I thought of all the Tribe boys as friends only. Warren finally said that he would go and have a talk with him.

I was wishing my oldest brother Jerry had been there. He had had lots of girlfriends and now he was married. He would have known how to talk to the Tribe boy; I was already worrying how Warren was going to handle the situation. Sure enough, my fears were validated in just a few minutes.

Warren came back into the house and ranted at me about what a liar I was! He said he asked the Tribe boy if he had kissed me and he denied it. He said that the Tribe boy had no idea why I would say such a thing! I was completely mortified! I told Warren again and again that I wasn't lying, but it fell on deaf ears. He said that I was just wishing that the Tribe boy had kissed me; how could he think that? I went to my room and had a good cry. I was frustrated with the Tribe boy, I was angry at my brother, and at the moment, I hated all boys!

I managed to pull myself together and go out into the kitchen and help Mom with dinner. She wanted to know what was wrong. I explained the whole scenario to her. She listened but had no advice to offer. She simply said that the Tribe boy would get over it. I wasn't even sure if my mother believed me. I couldn't stand having anyone think that I was lying; much worse was having anyone think that I wanted the Tribe boy to kiss me!

That was the end of me going to hang out with the boys. I decided that the best way to not get into a situation like that again was to stay away. I missed them and they probably wondered why I never went to their house anymore, but the oldest one knew and he probably wasn't ever going to tell.

CHAPTER 12

ROCKIN' AROUND THE CLOCK

I loved music! It's true that I didn't take piano lessons for very long as a child, but that did not change the fact that I loved music. If I could have listened to the radio from morning until night, it would not have been enough to satisfy my unquenchable thirst for any tune that made me feel like dancing. I would get a melody or lyrics into my head and go over them repeatedly until another tune would pop into my mind. It's amazing that I was able to learn anything in school with all the music going through my head! Sometimes I wondered if it was so loud that other people could hear it. I hoped not; I didn't want anyone to think I was a nut case!

There was so much music around me, I could not have escaped it had I tried. The radio woke me up on school mornings to KJR Seattle, Channel 95. It had the best music as far as I was concerned. The bus driver always had the radio on; he obviously had the same taste in music as the majority of kids on the bus. We suffered through classes, deprived of hearing the toe-tapping, hip-wiggling, dance-inducing music we all loved, but as soon as school was over for the day and we were back on the bus, the music started again. Once we were home from school, the television sets were turned on, and the afternoons were spent watching American Bandstand. Then I, and more than likely everyone in my generation, would go to our rooms to do our homework while listening to our favorite radio station.

Female vocalists sang Johnny songs. "Johnny Angel" was sung by Shelley Fabares, and Joanie Summers sang "Johnny Get Angry." Hayley Mills even got on the band wagon and sang "Johnny Jingo." Male performers would sing about the girls they obviously loved such as Sheila, Cindy, Patches, Sherry, and Diane.

Twisting songs were really popular and many different artists were singing them. Chubby Checker sang "The Twist" and "Slow Twistin'". Sam Cooke sang "Twistin' the Night Away," Joey Dee and the Starlighters sang "Peppermint Twist." Gary U.S. Bonds performed "Dear Lady Twist" and "Twist, Twist Senora." "Twist and Shout" was sung by the Isley Brothers.

We were invaded by the British early in 1964. On February 9, the Beatles made their American debut on the Ed Sullivan Show. I sat in front of our television with a girlfriend from next door, and the two of us screamed our lungs out with every note they sang! Gerry and the Pacemakers, the Dave Clark 5, and the Rolling Stones all converged on American soil within several months of each other. America's teenagers loved them all, and that included those of us on our little island in Puget Sound.

The Beach Boys and the duet of Jan and Dean brought surfing songs into the top 40 many times over. The Beach Boys became my favorite group, with the Beatles being a close second. My friend Cheryl and I had what I believed to be the experience of a lifetime by going to see the Beach Boys live in concert in the Opera House at the Seattle Center. Included on the ticket were Bobby Vinton, the Cascades, Trini Lopez, and Jimmy Gilmore. We screamed and laughed while the tears rolled down our cheeks. What a great time to be alive!

On Saturday mornings we could listen to the top hit songs of the week on KJR. Pat O'Day was the host and every teenager loved him.

He was as likeable as Dick Clark on American Bandstand. Needless to say, the years of 1962 to 1964 were incredible years for music and also for dances!

Chubby Checker rekindled the Twist with his movies and songs. He also introduced us to the Pony. Dee Dee Sharp introduced the Mash Potato, and then the Monster Mash by the Crypts came along about the same time as Halloween. Little Eva showed us how to do the Locomotion and sang a song that actually gave the dance instructions. A little later, in 1963, we were introduced to the Hitch Hike and the Monkey. Between watching the artists performing their songs and seeing their dances in the movies and on television shows, our generation had no problem finding a style of dance to accommodate even those rare individuals who lacked the rhythm or coordination to dance the sophisticated styles.

What was really fun at the movie theater in Lynwood was when a new dance was introduced. Back then Hollywood got in on the action and produced films that were actually made to teach the audience how to do the latest dances! When the music started and the artists began dancing, it was all we could do to stay in our seats and not fill the aisles and front of the theater with our bodies. Sometimes I would be seated in a row of seats that were not firmly bolted to the floor, so the seats rocked along with us!

I remember on one occasion, we got carried away by the music and dancing and couldn't help but get out of our seats and dance. The owner, who was like a father to all of us, came down into the theater and did his best to coax us back into our seats. He was having little success, so he went back up to the projection room and shut the movie off until we settled down! He then came back down into the theater, got up on the narrow stage in front of the large screen, and talked to us about how important it was that we stayed in our seats. He didn't want to alarm us, but he wanted us to know that we were much safer if we stayed in our seats. (Looking back, I realize that if anyone had gotten hurt, he could have been liable. Of course, back then people were not sue happy.)

The girl who babysat for us (that is my younger sister and brothers) was a cheerleader. Bainbridge High School was a small school and did not have the resources in either students or money to have separate cheer and dance squads. So, the cheerleaders got to do dances in their routines; it was fun to go to a game just to watch them; I loved their creativity. I knew that when I got to high school, I wanted to be a cheerleader too.

Dancing wasn't just a way to express how we felt about the music we listened to. For some, the love of performing was just inherent within us. That became very evident when we danced in the seventh-grade play. I cannot remember anything about the play, other than those of us who danced were villagers. The local ballet teacher was invited to choreograph a dance for us, and the other girls and I were hooked! We asked her if she would consider starting a beginner ballet class for older girls like us. She said the schedule was full for the year but that in the next season, when we would all be in the eighth grade, she would start a class for older beginners. We were thrilled! I was going to get one dream to come true, that of taking ballet lessons. Of course, I still had to get Mom to agree, which might prove to be daunting.

I had been given an extra little part in our dance for the play. At the end of the dance, I was to take a couple of backward, sliding steps, turn and do a curtsy to end the dance, and then scurry off the stage while looking very light on my feet. I must have succeeded in my little performance because Mom agreed to let me take ballet lessons. I could hardly wait to be in the eighth grade!

CHAPTER 13

SEVENTH-GRADE MIXER

On Fridays in the seventh grade, the boys and girls got together during their scheduled PE time to dance. We were instructed on how to do round dances, square dances, and a few ballroom dances such as the Waltz and Fox Trot. We were given no instructions on the modern dances performed daily on American Bandstand. However, we had a dance coming up in which we were supposed to show off to our parents what we had learned in our Friday dance class. The Seventh-Grade Mixer was an important social event.

We knew weeks in advance that the dance would be held. Girls began preparing well ahead of time, planning what they would wear, how they would get their hair styled, all the usual things a girl would do. I did not know if the boys planned ahead or not, not did I really care; I just knew that I wanted to fit in.

I asked Mom if I could get a new dress for the dance. I knew I was asking a lot because we didn't have a lot of money with so many children in our home. However, Mom surprised me by saying we would go shopping the week before the dance. We went shopping at the JC Penny Store in Bremerton. I didn't hold out much hope of finding a pretty party dress, so I was really pleased when Mom and I spotted the perfect dress simultaneously. We both dashed toward it from opposite ends of the dress rack. There, almost dead center on the rack, mostly hidden from view, was a beautiful champagne-colored dress. It had a full skirt, three-quarter length sleeves, and a detachable fur trim around the neck. It was the prettiest dress I had ever seen! It was on sale, so Mom said that I could get new shoes too; how lucky could I be? Then Mom informed me that on the following Saturday, the day of the dance, I could go to the beauty parlor and get my hair done!

I was thrilled; I so seldom got to get my hair done by a professional. Mom was really outdoing herself letting me get dolled up for the dance; it was a rare treat indeed! Of course, I had to phone my best friends and tell them about my exciting news. I knew that most of the other girls were accustomed to having new clothes and getting their hair nicely done, but it was like serendipity, much more than I ever expected.

Needless to say, the week went slower than usual. The best part of the week was practicing dancing in front of the television during American Bandstand. All the kids in our dance class knew that we would get to dance modern dances after we showed our parents the dances that we had had to learn. We were more interested in the cool dances and doing them well!

I remember very little about going to get my hair done that day. All I really remember about it was that Mom took me all the way to Lynwood to get my hair done by the lady who had done it for me when I first went to McDonald School. I had been happy with it then, so she figured I would be happy with it again. She was right; I loved my haircut and style!

That evening after putting on my new dress and shoes, I was standing in front of my mirror seriously studying my reflection. I wanted to look as perfect as I was capable of looking. I was actually pleased with what I saw; I felt pretty. The song, "I Feel Pretty" from *West Side Story* went through my head. Mom had come through for me, and I would always be grateful. I was so excited, I felt like I could burst. I turned around once more to make sure everything was perfect. Mom walked by my open door and said, "Stop looking at yourself in the mirror; you look ugly!"

I instantly backed away from the mirror and shut my bedroom door. I glanced again at the mirror and wondered what looked ugly; I couldn't see anything in particular that my mother could have been referring to. I felt awful; I no longer wanted to go to the dance. Mom had already made plans to meet up with the parents of one of my friends, and we were all going to the ice-cream parlor after the dance. I couldn't let them down when they were planning on a night of fun. I just had to go along and smile and act like I was having a good time.

The Seventh-Grade Mixer probably had a theme, but I don't remember what it was. I was in such a terrible mood and state of mind that it's amazing I can remember anything about the dance at all. I remember having to waltz backwards while the boys waltzed forward. I can still hear our parents laughing while they whispered to each other, "They're just moving in one direction!" I felt humiliated, like a fish out of water.

After we had gone through our entire repertoire, we were given the opportunity we had been waiting for. Our favorite current songs were played and we could dance the way we wanted. It was like being on American Bandstand, only our parents were seated at the tables surrounding the cafeteria floor. The teachers were manning the phonograph, standing there watching until they until they were coaxed onto the dance floor too. If only our parents would have joined us instead of sitting at their tables just watching. I think I might have had fun if I hadn't felt every parents' eyes on me while they were thinking what an ugly girl I was.

At least, it looked to me like everyone was having fun. I just wanted the entire evening to come to an end as quickly as possible. I usually enjoyed acting, always wanting to be someone else. However, on that night, I could not forget that I was me and that Mom had told me I was ugly. Try as I might, I could not pretend to be someone else and just have fun; it was useless.

The dance finally came to an end and good-nights were said. My parents and their friends said they would meet at the ice-cream parlor in a few minutes. I normally loved ice-cream, but that night it was just like putting salt into an open wound. I had to endure being around my friends and family even longer. I smiled and acted like I was having a good time. I ate my ice-cream although I can't remember what I ordered.

Later that night, when I was back in my room, I slowly took off the prettiest dress I had ever worn. Tears welled up in my eyes as I thought about the fun I could have had if I hadn't been worrying about being the ugliest girl at the dance. I knew that my dress was pretty and so were my shoes. I knew my hair looked good for once. But Mom had said that I looked ugly, and I had never known her to lie to me before.

I knelt beside my bed that night and poured out tears to God. I asked Him to take away my sorrow and help me to be able to be a good person and do the things He wanted me to do. I asked Him to make it possible for me to go to California to live with my father. I knew for sure that I wanted to go and live with him. It was a scary thought, but we had been writing to each other since the World's Fair, and I thought that I might be happier living with him; at least he didn't think I was ugly.

The next morning was Sunday, and I got up and dressed for church as usual. I knew that I was the only one in my family who would be going, but that was fine with me. I felt like I needed to be away from Mom and be at church where I had friends and where I felt loved and accepted. Sure enough, by the time the church service was over and I was entering my Sunday school class, the sadness of the previous night was gone. When people asked if I had had fun the night before, I could lie and say, "Yes, I did."

I thought it was better to tell a "white lie," than to tell the truth and make people feel bad. I went home and into my room, turned on the radio, and listened to some really good music. My cares drifted away as I imagined I was Venus in Blue Jeans. I really perked up when the Beach Boys came on singing "Surfin' Safari." The music that I loved would keep me going through the highs and lows of being thirteen.

CHAPTER 14

THE CHURCH MOVES

The final service was held in our wonderful old church on March 4, 1963. Emotions were at a height I had never experienced within our congregation. In a sense, it felt like being at a funeral. We were saying good-bye to our old building and had that sense of loss felt when someone you love passes on. At the same time, we were filled with anticipation and assurance that all would be well with the new construction and remodel of our dearly-loved church building. I likened those thoughts to the hope we feel at a funeral when we think about the resurrection. Yes, that was a day of sadness and a day of rejoicing.

After the church services were over in the morning, we convened at the new location for the ground-breaking service. As I was walking with my friends from church to the new location, it suddenly dawned on me that my walk to church in the future would be much shorter. The new location was really close to where the trail through the woods exited to the road. I knew that soon I would be able to walk through the woods and then just a little walk along the road to reach my destination. It was going to be so convenient; I could hardly wait.

My cousin Kenny informed me that most of the furnishings from the church were going to be stored in their barn. The pews were going to the Christiansen's old chicken house! I had to laugh at that; memories of Mom and me going to get a chicken for dinner rushed into my mind. It was hard to imagine the smelly old chicken house being suitable to hold our church pews. Of course, the chickens were long gone and the smell too.

The ground-breaking service was rather boring to me; I was anxious to get home. It was fun being with my friends, but I just wanted to get out of my dress and into comfortable clothes so we could really enjoy the rest of the day. I'm sure my friends felt the same way; wearing church clothes was rather inhibiting for fun activities. As soon as the benediction was said, we went our separate ways. Cheryl and I planned to meet near Grandma Henderson's and spend the rest of the day together.

Moving items from the church building took a couple of weeks. There was a lot to do in preparation for the move. The building had to be disconnected from its current location and the structure within had to be braced in such a way as to keep things stable during the move. It was fun to go and watch the men working and help whenever and however I could. I got to be a gofer several times; that meant I would "go for" whatever was needed.

Our Sunday services were being held at the Seabold Community Hall. I remember thinking that it must have looked similar when my dad attended school at the hall. When he was young, the hall had been the local schoolhouse. What a history that old building had! I hoped that it would never be moved; I loved it just where it stood! I had so many wonderful memories of that old building and could only imagine the memories that would be made in the future. Because of the increase in our extended family, our gatherings were often taking place in the hall. Holding our church services there did not seem strange at all; the hall was like a second home.

The morning of March 21st, at 9:00 a.m., the crews gathered for the big move. It was pouring rain, not unusual for the first day of spring. The power lines had to be disconnected and replaced after the building and the steeple were moved down the road to the new location. I wasn't there, but Mom actually went and was able to relate the events to me. The actual moving did not begin until 10:00 and by noon, the building was beside its new location. The next day, March 22nd, the church was put onto its new foundation. Luckily, that turned out to be a bright, sunny, beautiful day, befitting the occasion. The steeple was placed on top several days later. It drove me nuts that I couldn't be there and watch history in the making, but school came first. Every day after school, I would walk up to the new location and look at the transformation.

We continued to hold our church services in the Seabold Community Hall. However, most of the congregation was spending many hours at the new location helping with the remodel and the new addition. My cousin Judy and I had one of the most fun jobs I think we could have been assigned. We got to stain the new woodwork in the front of the chapel! There was a beautiful work of wooden arches in the front of the chapel, as well as the new pulpit and the wood around it. We got to stain for hours!

The remodel of the old church was completed on August 18th, and my cousin who had taught me to play the piano was married there on August 24th. Going to her wedding and watching her walk down the aisle to stand in front of that pulpit gave me a sense of accomplishment. I had helped in a small way to make something beautiful and lasting, something that would bring years of enjoyment to many people. It was a very good feeling.

CHAPTER 15

HALF WAY THROUGH

The end of the school year was fast-approaching. My friend Mary and I wanted to earn some extra credit in our science class. We had science in our homeroom with Mr. Wells, my mother's tenant. Mary and I approached Mr. Wells one day just as the class dismissed for the noon break. We told him that we wanted to make a thermometer for extra credit. His face lit up like he had just been plugged into an electrical socket. He was a very high-energy type of person normally, but then he acted as though he had just been injected with a massive dose of adrenaline. He was more excited than we were!

He immediately told us the dangers of working with mercury and that he would have to obtain special permission from the school officials because of the dangerous substance. He said that we would need notes from our parents saying it was okay for us to handle the mercury with adult supervision. We had no idea that there would be so many hoops to jump through just to make a simple thermometer!

The day of the project finally came. Mary and I had planned to spend the night together at her house so her mother could pick us up after school. Because it was an extra credit project, we had to remain after school hours to build it on our own time. Mr. Wells was only too happy to assist us. It was the end of the school day and a Friday as well, but that wasn't slowing him down in the least. He rolled up his shirt sleeves and said, "Let's get to work!"

We went to the back of the room where he had various science projects set up. Some were on display to encourage our creativity and interest. Others were half-done projects belonging to other students. Our project was going to be done in one afternoon because of the danger of using mercury.

Mr. Wells had some thin rubber gloves he put on to handle the mercury. Mary and I had no protective gloves. The liquid mercury was in a small glass bottle. It rolled around like a soft ball. I had never seen anything so strange. It was a liquid, yet it acted sort of like a solid; it was fascinating! Mr. Wells was going to pour the liquid mercury into a little glass vial that would be the bulb of our thermometer. Pouring was quite a trick because the mercury wanted to remain in its shape as a ball. The mercury rolled out of the bottle instead of flowing! Mr. Wells used his gloved finger to break the ball as it formed on top of the opening to the small vial. Enough of the silver liquid rolled into the bottom of the vial to meet our requirements.

With that task done, Mary and I could take over the rest of the project. I don't know how it happened, perhaps because the mercury is very heavy, but Mary picked up the vial and the bottom burst out. The mercury fell to the floor and separated into many tiny balls rolling every which way! We both let out a small scream simultaneously, and Mr. Wells must have jumped three feet; he was a very athletic man! He immediately said, "Don't touch it!"

We stood back, afraid of what might happen if we were to touch the poisonous liquid. Mr. Wells got a small hand broom and dust pan and scooped up the tiny balls. He emptied them into a garbage bag and tied a knot while explaining to us that he would have to make sure it was disposed of safely. He thought he may be able to take it to the Winslow Clinic and ask them to dispose of it. I didn't know about

Mary, but by that time, I was wishing we had not wanted to make a thermometer!

There was enough mercury left to have one more attempt at making the thermometer. Mr. Wells had another tiny glass vial, so we said we wanted to try again. The project went off without a hitch; we succeeded in making the thermometer, attaching a blank card behind it so we could mark the rise and fall of the mercury as the room heated and cooled. We couldn't mark freezing or really high temperatures, but we understood how the thermometer worked. We had also learned a lot about the dangers of the liquid metal, and we received an "A" on our project.

There was going to be a graduation party for the eighth graders. The seventh graders who wanted to help with the decorating were invited to remain after school on the appointed day. I had always loved to decorate for the holidays and our birthdays, so I knew that decorating for the eighth graders big event sounded too fun to pass up. There were quite a few of us who remained afterschool that day; I think we were all a bit envious of the eighth graders going into high school.

I was going to turn fourteen during the summer. I should have been going into the ninth grade instead of the eighth. I didn't talk about my feelings with anyone, not even my closest friends. I think most of my friends just thought of me as being their same age. I guess that was one of the blessings of being small and looking younger than I was.

On the last day of school, we were engaged in signing each other's year books, journals, and whatever else we had brought to school to make a lasting memory. Instead of being sad to say good-bye for the summer, we were filled with anticipation because we were now going to be eighth graders! We would be the big kids on the block; we were the upperclassmen! And, of course, we would see each other throughout the summer. The island wasn't very big, and there was only the one theater in Lynwood. We made plans to see each other on Friday nights at the movie. Summer would pass quickly enough, and it would be September before we knew it; we had made it half way through junior high!

When I got on the bus and took my seat, I looked around at the other kids. I looked at the eighth graders who were going into high school in September. I looked at my old friend who had abandoned me when I had to repeat the second grade while she went into third. I had seen her every now and then during class changes and other activities. She never acknowledged me, and I was still too hurt to try to rekindle the lost friendship. I was glad that she would be in high school so that I wouldn't need to see her anymore. I decided that I had plenty of friends and that this was going to be the best summer ever!

CHAPTER 16

COED CAMP

Most young people love to go away to summer camp; I was no exception. I had enjoyed going to Campfire Camp and Girl Scout Camp, but we could not afford for me to spend more than a week at camp, so I had to choose which one I wanted to attend. I was a devout Methodist by that time in my life, so the decision was easy; I wanted to attend the Methodist Youth Camp. That decision resulted in serendipity; my best friend Cheryl would be attending also and the camp was coed!

At church we were told a little bit about what to expect during our stay at the camp which was located out at Ocean Shores. Being a church camp, there would be morning devotionals and private time for scripture study or journal writing. We would have art projects and a talent show. Everyone was encouraged to participate in the talent show. Cheryl and I decided that we wanted to do an act of some sort together.

One day at Cheryl's house, we put our heads together and tried to think up an act that we could do well enough to not embarrass ourselves in front of our peers. Worse yet, would be to make fools of ourselves in front of the adults. We had to find the perfect song or skit that fit us to a "T."

It was Cheryl who had the brilliant idea of singing the song, "Let's Get Together." It was a song sung by Hayley Mills in the Walt Disney movie *Parent Trap*. Cheryl and I could pass for sisters. We both had dark blonde hair and were petite. Cheryl had brown eyes and mine were blue, but we knew that no one would be able to see our eye color from a distance. It was the perfect song for us.

We played her record over and over while we sang along, memorizing the words. Then we choreographed some cute moves to express the words of the song. We were on a roll! The challenge came in figuring out our costumes. We knew that we would probably be wearing jeans or another type of pants and a shirt for the evening anyway. We decided to make vests to wear over our shirts, sort of like Hayley Mills wore in the movie; we were ready!

As with all camping trips, even those to organized camps, we had to bring sleeping bags, air mattresses or foam pads, lots of clothes, personal hygiene products, reading material, and other individual wants. In other words, we had a lot of stuff! Luckily our food was provided and cooked for us. We went to our meals in the huge mess hall. The mess hall was one of the many places where we could mingle with the boys. The girls' cabins were on one side of the camp and the boys on the other. Needless to say, we wanted to mingle with the boys as much as possible.

One boy in particular caught my attention. He was tall and blond with blue eyes. I can't remember his name after all these years, but for the sake of this story, I will call him Brian. I could tell that he liked me from the moment we first met. He made me feel like Jell-O just like my first boyfriend had. I was a succor for boys that had good manners and big smiles!

Every day there was time set aside to swim or romp in the surf. The time was based according to the tide; so every day swim time had to be set slightly later than the previous day. It was on the second day of camp that I had a near disaster.

We had gone to the beach to play in the water during the designated time. One of the male leaders said that the surf was extra rough on that day so to please stay with other kids and look out for each other's safety. The leader would blow a short whistle when we needed to pay attention or two short whistles when someone was in trouble. A long whistle meant it was time to leave the water; it was very dangerous to stay in the water once the tide changed and headed out.

A group of us were together out romping in the waves. I had always been very buoyant and never worried about sinking. Unfortunately, that did not help me on this day. In fact, it put me into a very dangerous situation. The undertow suddenly became very strong, and I was pulled away from the group of kids I had been with. I yelled for help, but the sound of the crashing waves together with the wind made it impossible for anyone to hear me.

I struggled, trying to keep my head above the water while searching with my feet for a sandy bottom; I was failing at both miserably! I could see Brian's tall body above the waves, and I kept hoping that he would notice that I wasn't near him. I yelled again, and he actually turned to look to his side and saw I wasn't there. It was then that I saw him turn toward me. He didn't need to swim to get to me; he was able to take several long strides and reach for my hand. I felt his strong hand clasp around my wrist. By then I was so tired, I just gave up and let him hold onto me.

He kept yelling at me to try and walk toward him, but my feet couldn't touch the bottom. It was so scary; the waves were crashing over my head while the undertow was pulling my body outward toward the open water. The undertow must have been stronger than Brian because I began slipping out of his grasp!

He turned to yell for help and my wrist slipped out of his hand. I could not believe how quickly the distance between us grew. He was still standing in the same place, and I was at least twenty feet away from him within a couple of seconds! I was so buoyant that the current had full control of my body. I could see that help was coming; I saw two of the male leaders heading toward me in an oversized row-boat. They came right to me and reached over and grabbed me. They yelled for me to hang on to the side of the boat. I was so exhausted that I barely had the strength to do it. One of the men manned the oars while the other did his best to keep hold of my wrists. The boat headed toward Brian, and he grabbed hold of the back of the boat and let the boat pull us both to shore.

I could hardly stand up when we reached shallow water. Brian helped me walk onto the beach, and the leaders came with wool blankets to put around me and shield me from the wind. I had a good cry; I tried not to cry, but I just couldn't help myself.

After resting for a little while, Brian walked me back to my cabin. He asked if I was going to be okay, and I assured him that I was. He said that he would see me later at dinner. By dinner time I was feeling like my old self again, just extremely hungry. I'm sure everyone including Brian was amazed at the amount of food a small person like myself could consume. I was an active girl and I could work it off, especially when I got myself into predicaments like the one that afternoon!

The next day another memorable experience of that week happened once again on the beach. We were on a nature walk with one of the female leaders when I tripped on a branch that was protruding from the sand. I reached down to grab the branch and fling it as far away as I could, but as I lifted the branch over my head, I noticed a naked woman on the end! I was completely shocked and then amazed that nature could produce something that looked exactly like a naked woman strutting her stuff! I lowered the branch and carefully examined every detail. I informed my companions that I was going to take it back to the arts and crafts class later that day and saw off the long end of the branch. Then I was going to glue a sand dollar onto her head for a large-rim hat. I would then nail or glue her to a piece of flat wood or bark for a stand. She was a burlesque dancer and that was that!

True to my word, after the nature walk, I took that amazing piece of wood to arts and crafts. I did the few things necessary to make her a work of art and entered her in the contest! She won first place. I felt bad that she won such an honor because I had done very little to make her; Mother Nature had made her. My leader reminded me that I had had the eyes to see her when many other people had probably seen that piece of wood and never noticed the woman on the end.

(My mother loved that piece of art which had a place of prominence in her home for many years. When Mom moved away to Eastern Washington, my brother Jerry asked if he could have the woman. I was married and a mother by that time and had no use for her, so I said okay. My mother and brother have both passed away, and I have no idea whatever happened to the wooden woman.)

The night of the talent show finally came. There were not as many participants as I had thought there would be. As we watched the other campers perform their acts, I was becoming increasingly nervous. I didn't ask Cheryl if she was nervous; I didn't want her to get nervous if she wasn't. One of us had to be calm!

We performed our song without a hitch! "Let's get together, yea, yea, yea. Two is twice as fun as one!" We sang and danced and truly did have twice the fun. I don't remember if we were judged or not; if so, we didn't win anything or I would have remembered. It really didn't matter; what meant the most to me was being with my best friend.

Those were the highlights of my week at coed church camp. I never saw Brian again and never missed him. In fact, I had completely forgotten about him until I met a boy in California who resembled him. However, that is a story for another book!

CHAPTER 17

MORE TROUBLE ON THE WATER

The best thing about the month of August was the warmer water in Puget Sound. Most of the year the water was absolutely frigid! However, by August, the summer sun had worked its magic, and the water actually felt tolerable. In reality, the water probably just felt warmer because our bodies had adjusted to the low temperatures after swimming during June and July.

Mom was working at a drive-in restaurant in Winslow called Crazy Eric's. She only worked part-time, and I was making a little money by caring for my younger siblings. It was a win-win situation for both of us; she didn't need to pay an outsider to babysit, and the money I earned stayed in the family.

In the middle of the week, Mom would try to come home early to take us to Twin Spits. We always had huge extended family gatherings out there on Sunday afternoons, but because it was summer and it was the best beach we knew of, she wanted us to have some extra sun and fun. Mom could hardly swim at all, so she counted on me to watch my younger siblings and make sure no harm came to them. I had just turned fourteen and would be going into the eighth grade.

I was an accomplished swimmer, and although I was very small for my age and had no life-saving skills, she figured I could swim well enough to handle any situation my siblings might get themselves into. None of them were prone to go out very deep in the water because they couldn't swim. They were happy to stay in the shallow water and play in the sand on the beach.

Twin Spits was such a beautiful beach. It was mostly soft sand as far to the north and south as we would care to wander. The sand was also soft deep into the water, even during low tide; just the entice-ment for little children to go out further than they should!

There were some naturally-occurring sandbars on the beach, and as the tide would come in, the water would find a low spot between two sandbars and quickly fill with the incoming tide. We would love to play in the warm pools created; they felt like bathwa-ter. As the tide continued to come in and the pools converged into a larger pool, we would make our way higher up the beach and let the incoming tide fill another pool. This scenario played out again and again on a weekly basis; it became a regular routine. However, I learned a lesson one day about not letting anything concerning the beach become routine!

We arrived at the beach about one 1:00 in the afternoon. Mom had brought hamburgers, french-fries, and soft drinks from Crazy Eric's. We spread out our towels, sheets, and whatever else we had to sit on the sand and enjoy our lunch. My two youngest brothers were always so busy playing that they got sand into their food almost as soon as it was placed before them. It amazed me that they didn't care and would eat it with the little grains of sand rubbing on their teeth. I cringed at the thought, but Mom said it probably just helped clean their teeth.

After we had eaten our lunch, Mom settled down to read a good mystery book. I told the kids they could play on the beach or wade but that they couldn't go further out than their knees until I gave them permission. I was still very conscientious about the one-hour rule of waiting after a meal. I walked far out onto the beach near the water's edge and turned toward the kids and my mother. With the sun slightly to the back of me, I could easily keep an eye on the kids without the sun in my eyes. Mom was lying on a towel facing away from the water. My youngest brothers were playing in the sand about thirty feet away from Mom. My little sister Susy and brother David were closer to me in one of the newly formed shallow pools.

I had been wading in the shallow water just deep enough to cover my feet. I was walking up and down the beach, somewhat keeping an eye on my siblings, but mostly just enjoying the feel of the sun on my body. I was definitely a sun worshiper! I hadn't noticed that the tide was rapidly coming in. The water was warmed so much by the sun shining on the sand that the water crept up my legs without me realizing what was happening.

I glanced up and saw that Susy and David had joined my younger brothers higher up on the beach. I was walking on a sandbar that was already two feet beneath the surface of the water. That meant I was going to have to go through some deep water to get into shore. Normally, that would not have been a problem because I was a good swimmer, but the incoming current was strong! Just like at the church camp, my buoyancy became a hindrance. As I tried to swim to shore, I was carried in a southerly direction away from my family. I tried to walk several times, but I could not touch solid ground. I swam with all the strength I could muster, heading in a diagonal line toward shore. I finally succeeded in reaching waist deep water where I could manage to fight the current and walk up to dry land.

I must have been a quarter mile down the beach from my family. I wobbled along the beach, out of breath, and out of steam. I didn't dare tell Mom or my siblings what had happened. I didn't want to scare any of them, nor did I want Mom to think that I was irresponsible and not capable of watching the kids. I certainly didn't want to bring our fun days at the beach to an end because of my stupidity. No one had noticed my little escapade, and I never told a soul.

My recent bouts with strong currents should have made me perceptive to the unseen dangers lurking beneath the surface of the open water. However, I loved to swim and hang out on the beach. If the sun was shining and the day was warm, I planned to go for a swim, as some people would say, "Come Hell or high water."

One day my cousin Judy and I planned to spend the afternoon down at the beach near her house. There was a trail that zig-zagged down from her house to a boathouse and bulkhead on the shore. Her family had a large rowboat that was anchored off shore. The tide was about half way in when we arrived. We planned to swim for a while, eat our picnic lunch we had brought, and do a little fishing. We definitely had a fun afternoon ahead of us, or so we thought.

We knew from experience that it was best to swim during an incoming tide, so we wasted no time in drenching ourselves to get numb as quickly as possible so we could swim. Her beach was rocky, and the water was much colder than over the warm sand at Twin Spits. When I would go for a skinny dip at the beach near my house, I always waited until the tide had come in over the rocks to warm it sufficiently. Then I would just take my dip in the sheltered area between the beach house and the overhanging trees; it always felt reasonably warm.

The tide still had a long way to go before coming in far enough to be warmed from the rocks. We had plenty of time to swim, and we made the most of it. We knew that we wanted to fish during the high tide, so we decided we had better get out of the water and eat our lunch. We had loaded our towels, shoes, lunch, and fishing gear into the boat when the tide was lower. We only had to wade about knee deep out to the boat. By the time we decided to have our lunch, the boat was out over our heads. We each swam to opposite sides of the boat and climbed onboard simultaneously so as to not cause it to capsize.

We enjoyed a leisurely lunch and then hooked some bacon onto our fish hooks and proceeded to cast our lines. I was a terrible fisherman; I couldn't cast a line very far at all. I decided that it really didn't matter; I was really there just to have fun.

Judy got a nibble on her hook almost as soon as she cast her line out. Her rod was really bending with the weight of her catch; this was exciting. She reeled and pulled, reeled and pulled, and I knelt by with the net, ready to catch the fish as she pulled it out of the water. Were we ever surprised when a pink octopus came up attached to the end of her line!

It was just a little octopus; neither of us had ever seen one up close and personal! It was so cute. She unhooked it and gently let it back down into the water. Immediately the water around it turned dark blue. It had obviously let its protective ink color the water to obscure it from view. We never knew if it survived the unintentional ordeal we put it through.

With our thoughts and actions centered on the octopus, we didn't notice that the tide had changed and was heading out. We were anchored so our boat could only float as far as the cable would allow. However, Judy had to get home because she had chores to do, so we couldn't wait until the tide was low enough to safely walk ashore through the fast-moving current. We debated a few minutes on the best course of action and decided to swim for it!

We dove into the water, leaving our belongings in the boat to be picked up later when the tide was out. Judy had chores and needed to be home to do them. If not, she would get restricted, and then we wouldn't have any fun together for two weeks. We probably had made the wrong decision, but we had already dove in and headed away from the boat before we realized what a bad decision we had made.

The current was very strong and pulled us northward, toward the beach below my house and then toward the Agate Passage. Whatever happened, we knew we did not want to get pulled into the Agate Passage. The current through that narrow waterway was so strong, we would not be able to survive; we knew that!

We swam with every ounce of strength we had. The current was not only pulling us in a northerly direction but also pulling us out into deeper water. We were getting further away from the shore as we moved up along the beach. Just before the beach below my house was an area where the land protruded a little further out. It made a slight curve to the beach. The water was shallower and the current subsided slightly as we neared the protrusion. We were able to stagger to the beach and crumple like two wet gloves onto the rocks. We were absolutely exhausted.

After resting for a few minutes, we gingerly made our way over the rocky beach as we did our best to avoid the barnacles. By the time we made it back to where the boat was anchored, the tide had receded enough that we could walk out and retrieve our belongings! How could two girls have been so rash? I had always thought females were naturally more intelligent than our male counterparts. However, this occasion made me seriously reexamine my previous assumption. As in the past, we never told anyone the stupid thing we had done.

CHAPTER 18

BIG KIDS ON THE BLOCK

Eighth grade! My friends and I were the big kids on the block; we had finally made it to the top! I could see it in their faces and hear it in their voices; the emotions were so tangible it was as if we could physically wrap ourselves in them. Euphoria would be a very good description of what we were feeling.

I was assigned to be in the second to the top math class. The top math class was algebra; my class was considered pre-algebra. I wasn't sure what that meant. I knew that algebra had to do with formulas using letters in place of numbers, but actually none of it made sense to me. I loved regular math and was good at it; why couldn't they leave well enough alone?

I was in the top reading class, no surprise. It was the English class that filled us all with amazement. The teacher was a very young and extremely pretty woman. She looked like a movie star! She had a perfect figure 8 shape! I had heard that women were supposed to be shaped like an eight, but I had never actually seen one until I walked into her classroom. I noticed immediately and saw that the boys had noticed too! I had heard the expression many times, "he looked like a dog with his tongue hanging out." The boys looked like a pack of wolves with their tongues hanging out!

(As I'm recalling that day and writing this memory, it is making me laugh out loud. I will never forget the giddiness of those boys; they acted like they had died and gone to heaven.)

I cannot remember much about that English class. What I vividly recall is seeing our teacher sitting on the top of her desk, crossing her legs, and proceeding to read to us. While her head was facing down, I would glance around the room. The girls were looking at the teachers face, the boys were looking at her legs! I did tell my mother about it and she laughed. I can still remember her talking on the phone to one of her friends and repeating what I had told her. She and her friend were quite amused by the whole scenario.

There wasn't a lot of difference between being in the eighth grade and the seventh. I still wanted to sing in the choir, so we would march up the hill to the high school annex during the last period of the day. There were still intermural games being held during the noon hour in the gymnasium; I was particularly fond of volleyball and badminton. My nose had suffered no lingering bad effects from the previous year's contact with the volleyball. Art was still offered, though nothing I did ever again received the same recognition as my smoking collage of the seventh grade.

I think the most noticeable difference in my classmates was in their level of maturity, especially that of the girls. We had grown into young ladies. The boys were still boys; I would have been hard pressed to refer to them as young men. That being said, there were still a few who caught my eye.

I had crushes on several different boys at the same time. But, that's all they were, crushes; there was not a serious side to any of those boys. Good grief, most of them were only thirteen. On the other hand, I was fourteen and wanted a boyfriend. I was in love with being in love! I didn't want a puppy love; I wanted to be somebody's number one! I guess I had seen a lot of movies and read too many novels about teen romances. It seemed that in order to have a fulfilling life, I had to have a boyfriend.

My girlfriends wanted boyfriends too. The trouble was that the boys were not cooperating in the least! We all were experiencing the same problems with different boys. We liked a boy and wanted them to notice us; the boy we had our eyes on had their eyes on another girl. The other girl had her eyes on another guy. It was like being on an amusement park ride, with everyone spinning in opposite directions and once every so often, you would pass by the one you wanted to be near. It was extremely frustrating!

Rather than lose sleep over my dilemma, I chose to ignore it as much as possible and just have fun. I figured when the right guy came along, we would both know it!

The hardest part of being in the eighth grade came toward the end of the school year. I mention it now because I don't wish to single any one person out; it was just how relationships with classmates evolved over the course of the year. Students began to form cliques. I really didn't notice it much among the boys; however, it was among the girls that there were definite divisions taking place.

Girls who had been my friends for several years suddenly wanted nothing to do with me anymore. Girls who I had only befriended the prior year were also now avoiding me. I would have been devastated by the occurrence had I not noticed that it was happening all around me. There were now the "In Group" and the "Out Group." I was obviously a member of the latter through no fault of my own. My best and dearest friend Cheryl was still the same and was not included with the "In Group." We would be friends forever and that was a constant I could rely on in my rapidly-changing world.

My brother Warren was having problems. He got suspended from the high school for ripping out one of the students' desks that had been bolted to the floor and tossing it out an upstairs, classroom window! His excuse for his behavior was that someone didn't think he could do it; he wanted to show off his physical strength! Once again my brother reinforced my conclusion that males lacked the same intelligence as females.

In order to be allowed back into school, he had to have a psychiatric evaluation. Frankly, the school officials were afraid of him. The evaluation was to last three days at the Western State Hospital. He did not pass the evaluation and had to remain there for several months! I remember going with Mom to visit him. Mom and I were escorted into the TV/Rec room, and then Warren was escorted in to visit with us. He was fully clothed in his own clothes and not in a strait jacket as I had imagined. He was, however, in stocking feet; he said that they were not allowed to wear shoes.

We had hardly begun to have a conversation when Warren's face turned red, and the tears began to flow. He wanted out of there and to come home. My heart was instantly breaking; I could never stand to see Warren cry. Mom was trying to be brave; she had so much to deal with. She said that she would talk with his doctor and see if he could maybe come home for short visits to start. That seemed to calm him down, and then I felt a little more at ease. The whole scenario was overwhelming for me; I wished I had not gone with Mom.

Seeing my brother in that place made me wonder why he was like he was. I remembered when he had gone to live with my father in California. He had been gone over three years. When he came home, he seemed fine. Then, as the months went by, he began to revert to his old habits of relentless teasing, disobedience, and emotional outbursts. The episode at the high school had only been the frosting on the cake.

I wondered if I had some mental disorder lurking within me, waiting to show its ugly face at some unsuspected time or place. Warren was my only one hundred percent sibling; we came from the same two parents. Perhaps what was wrong with him was wrong with me, and it just hadn't appeared as of yet! Would some traumatic event cause me to suddenly go off my rocker?

I wrote to my father in California; I told him all about Warren, his escapade at school, his mental episodes, and about the Western State

Hospital. I expressed my personal fears that I might be a nutcase too and that the problem just hadn't manifested itself yet.

My father wrote back, expressing his sympathy about Warren and trying to reassure me that I did not have the mental problems that Warren had. He said that Warren had been born with problems and that he was sure it was due to the fact that my mother had drunk and smoked too much during her pregnancy with him. He didn't know for sure; he just thought that made sense.

The next letter I received from my father was really surprising; he had moved! He said that he had been wanting to get out of Los Angeles for a long time; it was just overcrowded and becoming quite dangerous. He moved back to Garden Grove where his family had moved when he was a teenager. It had changed a lot over the past forty years, but it still had the same small-town feeling to him. He was renting a room and bathroom from his old voice instructor. He shared the kitchen and living/dining room with a young couple. My father said that the landlady also had a bedroom in the house that she stayed in when she came to Garden Grove on business. Her room had two twin beds in it; she said that I was welcome any time.

I had pushed my wishes and longings for living in California to the back of my mind. I hadn't given it a thought for quite some time. Suddenly, in my hand, I was holding an open invitation to go to California. I wasn't ready to make that big of a change in my life right then. However, I began from that very moment to plan on moving to California for high school. The clique at school, the lack of a boyfriend, my constant worry if Mom thought I was ugly, and all the other ridiculous stuff a fourteen-year-old girl worries about, suddenly became insignificant when I thought about going to high school in California.

I had many reasons to stay right where I was on the island for now. I was in the eighth grade, and there was no sense starting at a new school where I wouldn't know anyone. I had just begun taking ballet class and I loved it! (Mom and I were keeping it a secret from Dad; she didn't want him to know that she was spending money on the class.) With Warren in the hospital, I could not put my mother through any more stress than she was already dealing with! She needed me to help however I could and that's what I did. I did not even mention to Mom that my father had extended an open invitation to me.

CHAPTER 19

THAT INFAMOUS DAY

There were no classes being held on November 21ˢᵗ and 22ⁿᵈ due to parent/teacher conferences. It was only one week prior to Thanksgiving, so I thought it seemed rather odd to be having a break from school with the Thanksgiving break so near. The weather wasn't very good, as was normal for the latter part of November. It seemed to me, the best thing to do that day was watch television. Mom was working at the Martinique Restaurant, and I was watching my siblings. As often as possible, I watched the kids so that Mom didn't need to pay anyone.

All the kids were immersed in their own activities, so I went into the little TV room next to my bedroom and turned on the television and sat down at 10:00 a.m. to watch a rerun of *I love Lucy*. I had always been an admirer of hers since my mother had told me that she was a stand-in for Lucille Ball during her early film days. Lucille Ball was not only a gifted actress, she was, in my opinion, the best comedian that I knew of. I ended up laughing so hard, tears were forming at the edges of my eyes. I could never understand why my siblings didn't think she was so funny; oh well, it meant I had the TV to myself.

At 10:30 a.m. *The Real McCoys* came on. It was an entertaining show and sometimes induced me to laugh out loud, but nothing compared to Lucy. The show had hardly begun when there was a breaking news bulletin. President Kennedy had been shot! There wasn't enough being said about what had happened, so I quickly changed the station. I changed the channel several times, trying to find a channel that would give me the information I was seeking. No one had any details! It was so frustrating. I finally settled in to watch CBS with Walter Cronkite. They had only recently begun broadcasting a half-hour nightly newscast. In fact, their first broadcast included an interview with President Kennedy! Since I was a fan of the President, I had become a fan of the *CBS Evening News*.

At first there was only audio coming from the broadcast. But after half an hour or so, I was able to watch Mr. Cronkite as he sat at his desk in the news room, wearing a white shirt and tie but no jacket. Helpers were handing him reports as he was trying to talk to the camera; it was live and it was awful! I couldn't believe my eyes or my ears; nothing so horrible that I was aware of had ever happened in my lifetime. I was instantly glued to the television. I forgot about my younger brothers and sister; nothing mattered to me but watching and listening to Mr. Cronkite. He was obviously distraught!

Mr. Cronkite couldn't relate the news fast enough. He no sooner read from one report, when another was being handed to him. He was given a photograph that had been received via a wire-transfer. It showed the President and Mrs. Kennedy seated in the back of a limousine and Governor Connally and his wife seated in front of them. The bubble top that would have normally been over the occupants was not there; the President liked to feel close to the people. Everyone in the photograph was smiling; they were enjoying the warm welcome of the Texas citizens lining the street. The motorcade had made two stops so that the President could shake hands with some Catholic nuns and then some school children.

Mr. Cronkite shared some information about how the President and governor, accompanied by their wives, were on their way to a huge facility in Dallas known as the Trade Mart. President Kennedy would be addressing the audience which was mostly comprised of civic and business leaders and their spouses. Only two weeks prior to this event, Mr. Adlai Stevenson who was our UN Ambassador was not given a welcoming reception in Texas; he was hit and spit upon. The President had been asked to forego this previously arranged trip because there was fear for his personal safety.

Bulletins kept being updated and repeated. It was difficult to wait for more news. I wanted to hear something good, such as the President was going to be okay, but that was not the case. The news became more depressing as his condition was declared critical. A secret service man had been heard to shout, "He's dead!" No one could say as to whom the secret service man was referring to.

Apparently, as the motorcade had made its way around the corner onto Elm Street, three shots pierced the air! The President immediately slumped forward, and Mrs. Kennedy got down onto the floor of the automobile to cradle his head in her arms. A secret service agent immediately laid himself over the occupants of the car as it raced away toward the Parkland Hospital, which was only a little over a mile away. They arrived at the hospital at 12:38 p.m., CST. Vice-President Lyndon B. Johnson was in the car following the President, but he was not shot.

Immediately after the shots had been fired, police officers rushed up a hill toward where the shots had come from. A man and woman were huddled at the top of the hill with a crowd surrounding them. No one at that time could say if they were suspects. They were, however, immediately surrounded by the secret servicemen.

Another bulletin came in saying that the White House physician had arrived and rushed into the Parkland Hospital. Mr. Cronkite announced again that President Kennedy had been shot in the head and that Governor Connally had been shot in the chest. The latest news from the emergency room of the hospital stated that both the President and the Governor were still alive.

Mr. Cronkite filled in a few moments between bulletins by informing us about other assassination attempts on other presidents. I was so worried about President Kennedy that those other facts went in one ear and out the other!

The news switched to Dallas, and the announcer, Eddie Barker, gave some background regarding the Dallas Trade Mart where the President was scheduled to speak. Security at the Trade Mart was thought to be the best ever; it turned out that it was all for naught. An unconfirmed report came in that the governor had gone into surgery and that a secret service agent had been killed! The President was still in the emergency room.

Early reports said that a man was arrested by secret servicemen, however, there was no official report.

The news switched to the Dallas Trade Center. The huge audience had joined in prayer for the President and governor. The Reverend Luther Holcomb said the prayer; he had been initially invited to give the invocation at the commencement of the gathering. It was so gratifying to see complete strangers bowing their heads and asking God to take care of our President.

KRLD station in Dallas again reported that the President was dead. The word they had was from a doctor who was on the staff. There were tears in his voice when he gave the reporter the news. However, the reporter said it was not confirmed and that we had to wait for official confirmation. Then the announcer introduced the Reverend Luther Holcomb; he said that it was official, the President was dead. The Reverend turned the microphone over to a Paster Dickenson of the largest Methodist church in Dallas to give a benediction. However, the announcer Eddie Barker stated that the news of the President being dead was still unofficial!

Mr. Cronkite was handed a report from Dan Rather which said that the President had died! Mr. Cronkite said that it had not been confirmed and that other reports were coming in saying the same thing. He said we could not believe the rumors; we had to wait for an official report. He said that Mr. Rather's report was probably reliable, but that it was not official.

It was reported that at approximately 1:00 p.m. CST, the priest Father Huber pronounced the last rites for John F. Kennedy. Mr. Cronkite kept repeating the same news. Each time a new report was given, a little more information was added. We were informed that the governor was actually shot in the right upper back and the inner left thigh.

The official announcement came about half an hour later during a press conference by the acting White House press secretary, Malcolm Kilduff. Then the tears flowed; I was absolutely devastated.

In the midst of my emotional absorption with the televised broadcast of the morning's events, the phone rang! I did not want to answer it; I was in no mood to talk to any of my friends. I just wanted to stay glued to the television set. However, I thought that possibly Mom might have heard the news and be calling, so I forced myself to leave the sofa and walk to the other end of the house to answer the phone. It was my mother and she was very upset. With tears in her voice, she asked, "Have you heard the news?"

I acknowledged that I had and was hard-pressed to tear myself away from the TV to even answer the phone. After her usual exclamation of, "Oh my God," she let the tears flow. I suggested that she come home from work. She said that the boss needed someone to stay in case anyone came into the restaurant. She said that as the news spread, the patrons finished their meal and left quietly; no one else had come in, but the boss was worried that someone might.

I told her everything was fine at home, the kids were being good, and there was nothing to worry about. I remember very little about the rest of that day other than watching television. I didn't want to miss a single second of the news story. It was the longest news broadcast I had ever watched; it lasted four days!

Shortly after the announcement of President Kennedy's death, Walter Cronkite began informing us of what had transpired during the past hour regarding the shooter, Lee Harvey Oswald. He had shot and killed a police officer named J.D. Tippit; there were many witnesses to the shooting. Before being shot, Officer Tippit had radioed the police dispatch requesting backup. At 1:22 p.m., CST, a rifle was found on the sixth floor of the Texas School Book Depository building. By 1:55 p.m. Oswald was arrested at the Texas Theater in Oak Cliff for the murder of Officer Tippit.

Mr. Cronkite again repeated the somber news of the tragic events of the morning. More pieces to the puzzle were added with each news broadcast. I felt sorry for Mr. Cronkite; he was visibly shaken and beginning to look very weary.

Mom came home from work early that afternoon. She made herself some coffee and came into the TV room to cry and mourn with me. We sat there, side by side, crying as though we had been personal friends of the Kennedys. The news broadcast would take ten second breaks every now and then for station identification and to let other local stations join in. I had no idea what that meant because all I saw was CBS.

By 2:38 p.m. CST, the body of President Kennedy, with his wife Jacqueline, was back on board Air Force One. Vice-President Lyndon Baines Johnson was then sworn in as the 36th President of the United States. Mrs. Kennedy had not left her husband's side since the shooting. She did, however, leave his side momentarily to stand beside Mr. Johnson as he was sworn in, but then she returned to sit beside his casket during the flight to Andrews Air Force Base near Washington D.C.

When the plane landed, the President's brother Robert Kennedy boarded the plane. Moments later, the casket of President Kennedy was removed through a rear entrance and loaded into a waiting US Navy ambulance for transport to the Bethesda Naval Hospital. Then Jacqueline, escorted by her brother-in-law, stepped out of the plane.

My heart ached to see that beautiful woman wearing her suit still covered in the blood of her dead husband. Mom and I put our arms around each other and cried together. Our grief was shared by millions of people who were also tuned into their televisions, witnessing the most tragic event we had ever seen on TV.

A few moments after the ambulance drove away, President Johnson and the new First Lady exited Air Force One. They went to stand in front of a podium where Lyndon Johnson made his first official statement. It was hard to catch all of his words, but he said something like this: This is a sad time for all people. We have suffered a loss, and for me, a deep tragedy. . . I will do my best; that is all I can do. He then asked for our help and for God's help.

No one wanted to leave the television set that day. I cannot remember what we prepared for supper or if we even bothered to eat. I don't remember going to bed, although I'm sure that I did. All I remember is watching television.

On Saturday, we watched news clips of the tragic events as they had occurred the previous day. We learned about Lee Harvey Oswald and his rapid arrest. He was charged with the murder of the President by 11:26 p.m. CST, the very day he performed the fateful deed. Mom said that it was very rare to find and charge a criminal so quickly; I didn't know about that, but I was sure she was right.

We spent the day in front of the television, learning more about the previous day's events. Words of condolences were being offered from officials around the world. It was such a sad time.

On Sunday, I went to church just as I usually did. There was an air of sadness so tangible that I could feel it all around me. Our thoughts and prayers were with the Kennedy family, especially with Jacqueline and her two young children. They were going to need the prayers of the citizens of our country as well as those around the world to get through the ordeal in which they still needed to pass.

Once home from church, I planned to be right back in front of the television. What a day that was! While I was at church, so much had happened! When I walked into the house, the first thing Mom said was, "Oswald is dead!"

What a shocker! Apparently during the transfer from the Dallas Police Department to the County Jail, Lee Harvey Oswald was shot and killed by a man named Jack Ruby. It had happened in the basement of the jail in front of live TV cameras.

However, the news of Oswald's murder did not take precedence in the television coverage. On Sunday afternoon (just after church for me) a crowd of about 300,000 people watched as a horse drawn caisson carried Kennedy's flag-covered casket down the White House drive past rows of soldiers bearing the flags of the 50 states. The procession then proceeded up Pennsylvania Avenue to the Capitol Rotunda. The only sounds were made by muffled drums and the click of the horses' hoofs.

Jacqueline, holding her two children by the hand, led the public procession. Plans had been carefully laid, many of which Mrs. Kennedy had requested. However, things did not got according to plan, and Jacqueline just did as she felt prompted. She walked proudly, holding her head high, in spite of the black veil that shrouded her face from view. She presented such a dignified and noble presence; she was definitely a first lady!

Mom and I watched in fascination as the public lined up to view the casket that lay in the Capitol Rotunda. All that Sunday and through the night, the mourners came to pay their final respects. The plan had been to close the rotunda at 9:00 p.m., but only about half of the crowd had managed to get in to see the casket. Jacqueline and the President's brother Robert made the decision to keep the rotunda open for the masses. Originally, there were two lines of mourners, one on each side of the casket. However, by 2:45 a.m., the military officials doubled the lines and then quadrupled them.

On the day of the funeral, I was up before dawn; I did not want to miss one second of the day's events. I grabbed a bowl of cereal and headed to the TV room; Mom was only a few minutes behind me. I could not have imagined a more lasting tribute to our late President than to see the crowd lining the route of the funeral procession. There was an estimate of one million people along the route from the Capitol, back to the White House, then to St. Matthews Cathedral, and on to the Arlington National Cemetery.

After Jacqueline Kennedy and her brothers-in-law, Attorney General Robert Kennedy and Massachusetts Democratic Senator Ted Kennedy, visited the rotunda, the coffin was carried out onto the caisson. Ten minutes later, the procession began, making its way back to the White House. As the procession reached the White House, all the military units except for the Marine Company, turned right off Pennsylvania Avenue and onto 17th Street. The platoon of the Marine Company turned in at the northeast gate and led the cortege into the North Portico.

At the White House, the procession resumed on foot to St. Matthew's Cathedral, led by Mrs. Kennedy and her brothers-in-law, Robert and Ted Kennedy. They walked the same route that John F. Kennedy and his wife had often used when going to Mass at the cathedral. This was also the first time that a President's widow had walked in the funeral procession of her husband. The two Kennedy children rode in a limousine following their mother, while the rest of the Kennedy family waited at the cathedral.

I don't remember any of the funeral service or even if it was broadcast. My next recollection, one that has remained imprinted on my mind, is of Jacqueline Kennedy whispering to her son, John John, after which he saluted his father's coffin. Mom and I both cried at the picture of that sweet little boy saying good-bye to his father.

The television cameras followed the caisson and a long line of black limousines passing by the Lincoln Memorial and crossing over the Potomac River. Many of the military units did not participate in the burial service and left after crossing the river. The line of cars leaving the Cathedral was so long that the burial services had already begun when the last car arrived.

At the end of the graveside burial service, Mrs. Kennedy lit an eternal flame to burn continuously over his grave. President Kennedy was buried exactly two weeks after he had visited the cemetery for the Veteran's Day memorial service. Our President was gone, but not forgotten.

My mother and I were both emotional wrecks. We had spent hours watching television, more than either of us had ever done before. We had cried together over an event that to us was the most tragic thing we had ever experienced. Mom and I had grown closer together during that four-day nightmare.

(Until my mother died, and now for me 50 years later, that was the saddest time in the history of our nation that I had experienced until September 11, 2001.)

CHAPTER 20

THE BIRDS

My mother was deathly afraid of birds. I knew of no logical explanation as to why she possessed such a phobia, but it was very real and manifested itself on many occasions. Being the kind-hearted person that she was, she pushed her fears aside to allow me to have a pet parakeet. My first parakeet, Pretty Boy, died when I was in the fourth grade. To this day, I believe my mother was responsible for his death. I know she didn't kill him intentionally; it was just a sad mistake of feeding him a piece of a banana. She felt as sad about his death as the rest of my siblings and I did. Three weeks later she surprised me with a new parakeet who I named Pepe.

Pepe was the joy of my life, and by the time I was in the eighth grade, the whole family adored the cute, little bird. He was exceptionally smart, or at least I thought so. I could leave his cage door open, and he would fly in and out as he pleased. When night came, he always flew to his cage and climbed in to sit on his swing for a good night's sleep. I would cover his cage, and we didn't hear a peep from him until I uncovered him in the morning.

Mom checked out a book about parakeets at the library because she thought I needed more information about training him. I liked him just the way he was, but I thought I should humor Mom because she really was working on overcoming her fear of him. She thought that I should either train him for free flight with a string attached to his little leg or clip his wings so that he couldn't fly very far. There was no way I would clip his wings; I thought that was cruel and unusual punishment! I tried tying a string to his leg one day; that turned out to be cruel also! The poor bird could only fly around in a circle and was obviously very unhappy.

I informed Mom that Pepe was going to have to be allowed to fly the way that nature had intended. She said that he could only fly in my bedroom. That was fine with me; then I could have him all to myself! Pepe moved in with me and was as happy as a lark.

In the mornings I would uncover his cage and climb back into my bed. Then I would softly call to him, and he would fly to the bump where my toes were sticking up under the covers. He would then run up the entire length of my body to my chin and begin kissing me on my lips. Sometimes he would hop onto my forehead and play with my hair. He would then hop onto my pillow and make kissing noises in my ear; he was very affectionate.

Mom seemed more at ease with Pepe in my bedroom; her fear of birds seemed ridiculous to me. I remembered when I was a little girl and the bat flew into her hair while she and Dad were wall-papering their bedroom upstairs. She had gone berserk and had never fully recovered; her fear of birds had been firmly cemented into her persona at that moment. I don't think she ever realized that a bat is not a bird. She was trying to overcome her fear but was failing miserably; then she heard about Alfred Hitchcock's movie, *The Birds*.

Mom loved to read mysteries and suspense books. Her favorite authors were Agatha Christie and Alfred Hitchcock. She didn't get to see the movie when it was playing at the theater, but one night it was going to be televised. She was so excited and asked me to watch it with her. I thought it rather odd that she would want to watch a suspense movie about birds, but I guess she thought it might help her overcome her phobia. She popped some corn and had bought some candy so that we could pretend we were at the movie theater. I hadn't watched much television with Mom except for the horrible four days we spent glued to the television when President Kennedy was assassinated. This time we were watching for entertainment and Mom went all out!

The movie came on late in the evening and everyone else had gone to bed. We sat in the little TV room with no lights on and pretended we were at the theater. We had the blinds on the east side of the room shut; that was the side that faced the road. However, the blinds on the south side of the room were open. It was dark outside and there was an open field on the other side of our apple trees, so we didn't worry about anyone looking in.

The movie began with a good looking man named Mitch Brenner going into a pet shop to buy a pair of lovebirds for his younger sister's birthday, but the shop didn't have any. He recognized a pretty girl from a previous encounter, but she did not remember him, so he pretended to mistake her for a salesperson. Her name was Melanie; she was infuriated when she realized that he had played a practical joke on her.

Melanie decided to purchase some lovebirds and take them out to Bodega Bay to surprise Mitch. She made the long drive out to where Mitch's mother and sister lived, but they were not at home. She let herself into the house and left the birds in their cage with a note attached. As she was leaving, Mitch caught site of her just as she was attacked by a seagull. He invited her to dinner, and she hesitantly agreed.

Melanie and Mitch had a "love at first sight" connection to each other. It was obvious that his widowed mother Lydia and his younger sister Cathy adored Melanie as well. She made friends with Annie, who was Mitch's ex-girlfriend and ended up staying the night at her house. During the night, Melanie and Annie were awakened by a loud thud; a seagull killed itself by crashing into the front door!

At Cathy's birthday party the next day, the children were attacked by seagulls and the following evening, sparrows invaded the Brenner home through the chimney. The next morning Lydia went to visit a neighboring farmer who had had trouble with his chickens. She discovered his body, with his eyes pecked out; she fled in terror!

By this time, I was eating popcorn without even tasting it; with my eyes glued to the television, I was consuming handfuls out of sheer terror. Mom was making little moaning noises, but she didn't say anything, so I ignored her. The movie continued.

Lydia became concerned about Cathy's safety at school, so Melanie drove there and waited for class to end, totally unaware that a huge number of crows were gathering nearby. When she finally noticed that the playground was filled with them, she warned Annie, and they evacuated the children. However, the movement of the children caused the crows to attack, injuring several of the students.

Melanie and Mitch met for lunch at a local restaurant. A few of the patrons described their own encounters with the birds. While that conversation was taking place, the birds outside the restaurant suddenly attacked the passers-by.

My mother had been filling her mouth with candy. I could hear her breathing deeply, and I knew that the movie was upsetting her. However, I didn't want to start a conversation and miss any of the action; she was just going to have to get through it on her own. The onslaught of attacks from the birds continued.

At a nearby gas station, a motorist was attacked by the birds while he was filling his car with gasoline. He was knocked unconscious and the gasoline poured out onto the street. There was a salesman from the restaurant who was not aware that he was standing in a puddle of gasoline and he lit a cigar and dropped the match. The gasoline exploded into flames, killing him!

By this time, my mother was terrified. Her exclamations of, "Oh my God," were being replaced by a string of four-letter words.

The movie continued with patrons leaving the restaurant to survey the damage caused by the explosion and being attacked by the birds. Melanie was forced to take refuge in a phone booth until Mitch rescued her. When they returned to the restaurant, a hysterical mother accused Melanie of being "evil" and causing the attacks. Melanie and Mitch then returned to Annie's house and found her dead; she had been killed by the birds while pushing Cathy inside to safety.

Just when we thought the movie could not get any worse, there was a sudden thump on the window! Mom let out a scream that could have been heard in China! She grabbed my arm and dug in her fingers; I didn't know what to do! She had me in a vice-like grip as she exclaimed, "My God, they've trained those birds to attack people, and now some have been let loose!"

I could see the whites of her terrified eyes from the light of the television; she really believed what she had just said. I uncurled her fingers from my arm and told her that she was being ridiculous. We continued to watch in horror!

At the end of the movie, Melanie and the Brenners barricaded themselves inside the Brenner home. The house was then attacked by waves of birds, which almost broke in through the sealed doors and windows. During the night, between attacks, Melanie heard noises upstairs. She did not want to bother anyone, so she went up to Cathy's bedroom and opened the door. Birds attacked her, trapping her in the room until Mitch came to her rescue. Mitch insisted that they get her to a hospital. Birds gathered around the Brenner home as Mitch prepared Melanie's car for their escape. The movie ended in a weird way; the Brenners, with the lovebirds and Melanie, slowly drove through thousands of birds that nonchalantly stepped aside to let the car pass.

When the movie ended and I could actually breathe again (I always hold my breath when something scares me), I said good-night to Mom and went to bed. I felt sorry for her having to climb the stairs up to her bedroom; I'm sure that she turned on every light in the house on her way up.

The next morning, out of curiosity, I went outside to see if there was a bird lying beneath the TV room window. Sure enough, a robin lay dead on the cement walk. I went inside and told Mom and Dad. Dad immediately got up from the breakfast table and went outside to investigate and probably to dispose of the remains. Mom, on the other hand, grew more terrified and expressed her concern that our neighborhood would then be overrun with killer birds.

I think that Mom had wanted to watch the movie to help her get over her fear of our feathered friends; instead, it had the extreme opposite effect on her. However, she never complained about Pepe; he stayed in my bedroom away from my terrified mother.

CHAPTER 21

HERE WE GO AGAIN

One Saturday morning I was awakened by the sound of voices coming from the kitchen. I was not ready to start the day and really didn't want to listen to the loud conversation. However, because of their raised voices, I had no choice but to unintentionally eavesdrop on what probably was meant to be a private conversation.

Dad was normally a very soft-spoken man who seldom lost his temper. Mom, on the other hand, lost her temper often, was quite loud, and used very colorful language to express her feelings. On this particular morning, Mom's voice was quite muffled and Dad's was booming!

"I am not going to haul your junk down to the other end of the island again! Good grief woman, how many times do you need to move? Why do you need to keep all that junk? You keep adding to it, year after year, and then expect me to do all the work of hauling it back and forth according to your whims! Well, I'm not going to do it!"

I could barely hear Mom's voice now. I could tell that she was crying. I could hear enough to make out her quiet sobbing. She spoke a little louder and I could plainly hear, "I won't ask you to move again;

this will be the last time. It's just too hard for me to be so far away from the apartments and take care of collecting the rent and fixing things when they break."

"Fixing things!" Dad's voice boomed again. "When did you ever fix something when it broke? You will have me running around playing handyman when I need to go to work in Seattle every day! What am I supposed to do, work all day and then come home and work all night?"

Mom sobbed some more and through her tears said, "No, I will take care of the apartments. I will hire someone to work for me as a side job so that he doesn't expect full-time work. I just really need to be in Fort Ward; I have so many apartments there and only one house here."

Now I was all ears, listening carefully so as not to miss any part of their conversation. Mom was thinking about making her life easier, but what about the rest of us? Would she even think to consult with us? I loved living here in the big house; I did not want to move back to Fort Ward. I had lots of friends on the south end of the island, and because I was in junior high, I attended school with all of my friends on the whole island. But what about David and my little sister Susy? Was it fair to them to keep switching them from one school to another? My youngest brothers were not in school yet, so they didn't even enter into the scenario.

While I was lost in my thoughts, the voices in the kitchen had both softened, and I could no longer eavesdrop. I needed to get up and go into the kitchen to investigate and find out what was happening. I wondered if I should bring up the fact that I had over-heard their conversation. I didn't want to add fuel to the fire, but I did want to know what decision had been made, or if they were still thinking about it.

I got out of bed and made a quick dash to the bathroom. Once my morning ritual was completed, I went back to my room to get dressed and to pay attention to Pepe because I had seriously ignored him that morning. He was always so sweet and forgiving. He never held a grudge; he had at least a dozen kisses for me before going to work on his breakfast. His cage door was open, so I made sure that my bedroom door was securely closed so that he wouldn't escape and fly through house causing Mom more stress than she was already experiencing.

I walked into the kitchen as nonchalantly as possible and said, "Good morning!" Mom was seated at the kitchen table, a cup of coffee in front of her. Dad was standing between the table and the kitchen sink. He was visibly annoyed, to say the least. Even though Mom was the one who had been crying, I felt sorry for Dad. He had no tears, but his face was white and he was breathing hard. I thought he may have a heart attack!

I walked over to the cupboard and grabbed a box of cereal. I said, "I couldn't help overhearing your conversation earlier; are we moving?"

Dad was the first to respond with, "I guess so. Your mother seems to think that she is some sort of highfalutin landlady and that she has to be near her rentals." With that, he walked out of the kitchen door and went down the back stairs, obviously heading to the basement where he could putter away on something to take his mind off his troubles.

I looked at Mom with the question in my eyes; I didn't need to ask anything. "Yes, we are moving back to Fort Ward," my mother said. "We will be living in the south side of the big duplex across from where you worked last summer."

I had been inside once when Mom went to visit her friend. The square footage of only one side of the large duplex was far more than our big house in Seabold. I liked big houses; this would be fun. I had been worried that we might be moving back to the Parkview Apartments. After the motel experience, I had had enough of those crowded conditions.

With my mind at ease, I supposed the next hurdle for Mom was to let the rest of the family in on the news. I cannot even remember how she told them or what their reactions were! I was concerned about my ballet lessons and how we were going to continue to keep that a secret from Dad.

Several more days went without further mention of the impending move. However, I did receive a phone call letting me know that Ballet class was canceled until further notice! The Bainbridge Review building had burned down, not all the way to the ground but enough that it was useless for its current tenants. All the Ballet classes were held in a studio up on the top floor, overlooking the ferry dock and Eagle Harbor. The teacher had to find a place to rent that was large enough to house her classes; it would take a few weeks at least.

Oh my goodness! The church had moved, we were moving, and the Ballet school had to move. Mom always had said that things happened in three's; I guess that was proof enough.

Each June, the Ballet school held a dance recital. Our teacher planned for the coming June to be no different. She had already begun choreographing dances to be performed in the recital. We no longer had our huge room atop the Review building in which to practice. The only place the teacher could find to lease was the old Martinique Restaurant across the parking lot from the IGA grocery store. Besides being much smaller than our previous location, we also had to contend with a couple of vertical beams in the center of our improvised stage! Our teacher was managing with the less than ideal conditions, so we did too! Through carpooling, Mom and I managed to keep the lessons a secret from Dad.

We had made the move back to Fort Ward without a lot of fuss; we were old pros at moving by that time. I became good friends with the daughter of the deputy sheriff; her family was renting from Mom. We were in the same grade at school and liked the same music. Together we watched the Beatles perform on the Ed Sullivan Show, screaming our lungs out in front of our television. Even my little sister, as young as she was, liked the Beatles!

My friend Cheryl and I went to a Beach Boys concert just a couple weeks later. We screamed just as much, if not more than when I had watched the Beatles on TV. Even though we had moved back to Fort

Ward, Mom made sure that my friend Cheryl and I could still get together often.

Living on the south end of the island made it easier for me to rekindle close friendships with girls I had met in the sixth grade at McDonald School. However, the real benefit was being only a bike ride away from my current crush! The poor guy was riding his bike up to Fort Ward to see me at least a couple of times per week. Mom kept saying, "That poor boy; he's going to wear himself out." He did phone me now and then, but he seemed to enjoy coming for a face-to-face visit better. That was fine with me; I liked him a lot!

We would sit together on the porch stairs and just talk. I can't remember anything that we talked about, so it must not have been important. However, I will never forget the day he finally gave me a bear hug! We had just climbed down the stairs to the sidewalk where his bike was parked. All of a sudden, he turned to me, put his arms around me, and squeezed me in the best bear hug I had ever had! Of course, I hugged right back; in fact, we remained hugging for quite some time. I was hoping he would kiss me, but he didn't.

When we finally disconnected, he was grinning ear to ear; I'm sure that I was too. My heart was beating fast, and more than likely, my face was red. I could feel the warmth in my cheeks; I wished that I would outgrow the tendency to blush! He said that he would see me at school and then away he rode. I thought that that was the beginning of a serious relationship. Unfortunately, that was not the case. At school the next day, he avoided me! I thought he may be a little embarrassed, so I just smiled at him; he smiled back and I thought things were fine.

Sadly, he never phoned me again, nor did he ride his bike up to Fort Ward to visit me. I missed him terribly and wondered why he suddenly wanted nothing to do with me. When I would see him at school, flirting with other girls, my heart would ache. He became another item to add to my list of reasons to move to California.

CHAPTER 22

WHAT'S A MORMON?

I had continued to correspond with my father. He had moved to Garden Grove, California, and now he had another surprise; he was investigating the Mormon Church! He said that he had been invited to sing for their Sacrament meeting and, of course, he could not refuse. He informed me that his neighbor on one side, the people across the street, the people behind his house, and some people a few doors down the street were all members of the Mormon Church. He said that he felt surrounded by them and was very happy about it.

I didn't know what to think! I was a Methodist and loved my church. I knew that my father's grandfather had been a Methodist minister; my father had told me that in one of his earliest letters to me. My father had never really felt any loyalty to the Methodists; he just went to a convenient church when he felt in the mood. Now that he had been asked to sing, he was hooked; I read it between the lines! He loved to sing and had been semi-professional years before when I was a baby. He said that he had to overcome a few things before he could be baptized, but he hoped to become a member by the 4th of July!

I had never heard of the Mormons; I didn't know what kind of religion they were. I immediately went to ask my mother if she had ever heard of Mormons. She told me that as an infant, while we still lived in California, I had been blessed in the Reorganized Church of Jesus Christ of Latter-Day Saints. She said that at the time, my father had wanted to join that church. Mom didn't know the differences between the Reorganized Church and the regular Mormon Church; she only knew that the name of Mormon was a nickname.

Mom suggested that I go to talk with my Methodist minister. That was a problem because I now lived in Fort Ward and he lived in Seabold. I seldom got to attend church since our move; I just didn't want to attend a closer church. Mom said to call and make an appointment to see him. I was very surprised by Mom's interest; she really cared very little for religion. However, she was as curious as I was.

I went to see my minister on a weekday after school; did I ever get a surprise! As soon as I asked what he could tell me about Mormons, he was up out of his chair and pacing the floor! He wanted to know why I was interested. I told him that I was thinking about going to live with my father who was planning to join the Mormon Church. He looked at me with the most intense look I have ever seen coming from a man and said, "Stay away from them; they worship the devil!"

His statement took my breath away; of all the things my father had told me, he had not mentioned that very important piece of information! My mouth went dry and my heart began beating rapidly. I said that I had no intention of joining the Mormon Church. I was a strong Methodist and nothing would ever change that. However, I did feel like I should help my father see how mistaken he was and get him to come to church with me. My minister just shook his head and said, "Don't do it; if you go, they will utilize every possible means to get you into their church."

I felt dizzy as I left his office and went to meet my mother who had come to pick me up. She was as anxious to hear what I had been told, as I was to relate the information to her. I told Mom that I wanted to go to live with my father; I felt like I needed to save him from the devil worshipers! Mom said she didn't think that was a good idea. However, if I wanted to go for a short visit, she could see no harm.

The plan was set in motion; I would go to California for the month of August. However, I planned to stay if I liked being there; I figured it would take me more than one month to convince my father of the error of his ways. We had friends who spent their summers in Fort Ward and lived the rest of the year in Buena Park which was only about ten miles from where my father lived. However, August was a long way off, and a lot could happen before then. I still had to finish the eighth grade and have some summer fun.

Warren had come home from the hospital and moved with us to Fort Ward. I told him what my minister had said about Mormons, and he said that he had a friend who was a Mormon and that they did not worship the devil. That eased my mind somewhat, but I still worried. I was in a quandary because a man whom I had the utmost respect for had told me something very scary about Mormons, and yet my brother said that it wasn't true. Warren had always teased me while we were growing up, but he seemed very serious then; I knew that I would have to go and see for myself.

I began asking everyone I knew for information about the Church of Jesus Christ of Latter-day Saints; none of my friends had ever heard of it. I looked it up in the encyclopedia. It was founded by a man named Joseph Smith in 1830. The church's headquarters were in Salt Lake City, Utah. The president of their church was referred to as a prophet. The church had a little over half a million members, however, I was reading from an old encyclopedia. A small percentage of the members had practiced polygamy until their fourth president, Wilford Woodruff, put an end to it. Young men gave two years of their lives to serve as missionaries, putting education and careers on hold.

Wow! Needless to say, that was impressive. The article said nothing about worshiping the devil, although it did state that many people falsely accused them of belonging to a cult. The article said that they believed in God the Eternal Father, in His Son Jesus Christ, and in the Holy Ghost. I was reading from an old encyclopedia; the question going through my mind was, "Could the book be wrong?" How could the encyclopedia have said something so different from what my minister had told me? I was definitely going to have to go to California and see for myself. I would rescue my father if I could; or maybe, leave well enough alone and let him be.

CHAPTER 23

EIGHTH-GRADE GRADUATION

At the end of a school year, there is always a flurry of activity. Even my first year of the second grade, when I had actually only attended school a total of three weeks, the end of the year brought many extra things to do. However, no year-end activities thus far could compare with the vast array of social activities that I encountered at the end of eighth grade.

Mom and I had managed to keep my ballet lessons a secret from my dad. I don't know how we managed to keep him in the dark for nine months! Even though we moved from one end of the island to the other and had to scramble to adjust our schedules to facilitate me getting to and from my lessons, he never had a clue! Mom and I were both filled with anticipation over my pending ballet recital; we were curious to see how my dad would react when he saw me dancing.

Needless to say, the day of the recital, I was a bundle of nerves. Mom and I planned to keep Dad in the dark until I was on the stage performing. We told him that we were all going to my friends' ballet recital and that the cultural activity would be good for him too. He laughed at that but was such a good-natured, willing soul that he said he could fit it in to his busy schedule. That very act on his part, endeared him to me; he really was a good dad.

One of the other ballet students in my class lived a short distance from me. Mom took me to her house a couple hours ahead of when my family would be going. We told my dad that my friend was in the recital and that I was going with her to do her hair up for the performance. My dad believed the story; I guess we were very good liars. As soon as I arrived at my friend's house, we hopped into her car and her parents took us to Commodore Bainbridge School. The recital was going to be held on the same stage that we had performed as villagers in the seventh-grade play.

When we arrived at the school, my friend and I went into the girls' locker room. It had been transformed into a dressing room for the older girls. There were many classes getting ready for their performance, so many dressing rooms had been created for our special event.

Amid nervous giggles and laughter, the other girls and I proceeded to fashion ourselves into Ballerinas. Prima donnas we were not; we were just simple island girls who hoped to impress our parents. We helped each other put our hair into ponytails and then twisted them into buns. A few of the girls had bun-makers that we could actually roll the hair onto and fold it up into a bun; that was such a helpful gadget. I only had the old-fashioned rubber band, bobby pins, and hairnet. Luckily, I had a full can of hairspray; with my fly-away hair, I needed as much as I could get!

We even got to wear makeup. Our ballet teacher didn't want us to look made up; she wanted us to look natural, but also with enough added color that we wouldn't looked washed-out under the stage lights. We really loved making up ourselves and each other; I always enjoyed playing the part of someone else and this seemed no different.

When the time came for the performance, we all began going over our dance in earnest. We stood out in the hallway, in a circle, bent toward one another as though we were football players planning our next move. For us, it was every bit as critical. We talked the choreography through from the beginning to the end. We did not want anyone in our dance to make a mistake; we were in this together and we wanted to do our best.

One of the mothers came out to get us. "You ladies are on next. Go up the stairs and wait silently during the applause. When the other class has left the stage, make your entrance." The old familiar dry mouth and rapid heart rate began again. It seemed so odd to me that I would have such a reaction when I was about to do something that I thoroughly enjoyed. I hoped that my face wasn't red; no one could see my racing heart or dry mouth, but they could easily see my blushing face. I hoped the day would come that that would no longer be a problem; the sooner, the better!

We silently climbed the stairs and stood in the wing of the stage. The music ended, the applause thundered, and the girls rushed off the stage into the wing where we were waiting. As the last girl entered the wing, we did our little running steps out onto the stage and got into our starting positions. Even though the stage lights were bright, I could see out into the audience. There, right in the front row, dead center, were Mom and Dad. Dad's mouth was open and he had the most startled look on his face; he was every bit as surprised as I thought he would be.

As the music commenced, we began to dance; all else was forgotten. We felt the music carrying us through the choreography. We didn't need to concentrate on the routine; we knew it by heart. Whenever our eyes met, we would give each other a little smile of acknowledgement and encouragement. We danced as flawlessly as we were capable of. When the final notes began to play, we ended with a curtsy which we held until the music ended. Upon standing up, I looked directly at Mom and Dad. They were vigorously applauding and Dad was smiling; he wasn't upset that I had taken ballet lessons.

We took another bow and silently rushed off the stage into the wing. Without a sound, we scurried down the stairs and out into the hallway. Silently we scampered down the hallway to our dressing room, and then our emotions overcame us. We laughed and cried as we hugged and praised each other for a job well done. After we got that burst of emotion out of our systems, we went back to the entrance to the stage to wait for the curtain call when all of the students would be on the stage together. Someone gave a huge bouquet of roses to our instructor; we joined in with the audience in applauding her hard work.

When the final curtain closed, bedlam broke loose on stage, and we were all anxious to get out of there! I managed to find my way down the stairs and back to our dressing room. I grabbed my things and headed out to find my parents. I spotted my mother immediately and ran up to her, "Did you like it?" She said, "It was fine."

I really expected more of a response from her. I couldn't tell if she like the recital or not, nor could I tell it she liked my performance. Dad had gone out to the car; he didn't like crowds of people. As I approached the car, he was looking at me with a huge smile on his face. I had to ask, "Did you like it?"

His one word answer of, "Yes," said all that I needed to hear. It was in the tone of his voice and how he was smiling; I felt on top of the world!

We drove home in silence; I guess no one knew what to say. I was wondering if Mom had liked the performance or if she thought I had wasted her money. Dad was always quiet, so that didn't surprise me. However, on that occasion, I wished that he would have spoken up; I needed someone to break the ice. I mustered my courage and said, "Thank you so much for the ballet lessons; I learned so much."

Mom said, "That's nice."

She did it again; I didn't know if she liked the recital or not. I didn't have time to dwell on the subject because I had other things to occupy my thoughts. I had to study for finals and our graduation was next week. It had been scheduled a few weeks before school was out, even before our final exams! Mom had bought me a new dress a few weeks before, and I was anxious to wear it for the big night. I thought it was really cute, but I wondered what people would think of how it looked on me. I always seemed to worry about what everyone else thought.

Finally, the Friday before our graduation came, and with it, feelings of euphoria. We had made it through eight years of school. To us, it seemed like quite an accomplishment. I, of course, had repeated the second grade, so I had made it through nine years! Perhaps, I should not have thought in those terms; after all, I had only gone about three weeks during my first round of the second grade. However, I was every bit as thrilled as my friends and looking forward to being in high school.

Saturday night was the big celebration to which our parents were invited. The cafeteria had been transformed into a huge dance floor, surrounded by decorated tables that would seat eight. The buffet tables were on the side of the kitchen facility. Heavy hors d'oeuvres were displayed on the tables in smorgasbord fashion. Of all the times to be wearing a white dress; so many of the dishes looked like they could make a lasting stain if I were to accidentally drop something. I knew that I would have to be a very careful and dainty eater that night!

After we had eaten our dinner, the graduation ceremony began. Unfortunately, my last name was Van Pelt which put me near the end of the alphabet. I had to wait a very long time before my name was called and I could make that long walk up to the front of the room to receive my "hard-earned" diploma. Immediately after sitting back down on my chair, I slipped the ribbon off of the scrolled paper and unrolled the document to read it. "Friends, Romans, Countrymen, Lend me your ears. Look who is leaving the building after all these years. Vicki Van Pelt. Eight years you've gone, now four to go. So start low with a sigh, best of luck at Bainbridge High."

I had to laugh; the diploma was actually quite meaningless for me because I did not plan to attend high school on Bainbridge Island! If things didn't work out in California, I would come home and go to Bainbridge High with all of my friends. However, I was hoping to start a new life in California, attend high school in Garden Grove, and somehow get into acting. I knew that I had no chance at all of becoming an actress if I stayed on Bainbridge Island; I felt I needed to be closer to Hollywood. I loved to sing, to dance, and to act. Of course, my dreams were only the dreams of a fourteen-year-old girl. Life was full of surprises, and there had been many twists and turns to mine already.

Finals were no big deal. Some of the teachers had just wanted to scare us and keep us on our toes (so they said). Their year-end tests were fun, humorous tests that had little to do with the subjects we had been studying. It turned out that they had already graded us and decided if we passed or failed.

During the latter part of the week, we turned in our books, autographed friends' keepsakes and albums, and tried to endure the overwhelming sense of being a racehorse at the starting-gate. All of us were looking forward to summer fun and, of course, going to high school.

CHAPTER 24

SUMMER FUN

I couldn't believe it; school was out and I had three months of freedom! I had no job prospects for the summer months; I would have been lucky to get any babysitting jobs. I was too far away from the strawberry fields to pick berries; it was hot work and I tended to get heatstroke easily, so it was just as well. I knew I would have to figure out a way to earn some money so I could buy new clothes and things for school. I would need them in California just as much, if not more than on the island.

Of course, I expressed my concerns to Mom and she said that she would pay me an allowance to keep the house clean and cook dinner. That was a help, but not enough (although I didn't mention that to her). I just thanked her and said that I would do my best. Mom was working on the ferryboat, the Winslow to Seattle run. I thought that was so funny because she was deathly afraid of water deeper than her waist, she could hardly swim, and she became seasick so easily! She often told me stories of having to run to the ladies' room because of seasickness every time the weather was rough.

I shared the top floor of our huge duplex with my brother Warren. I had the big bedroom which faced south. I set Pepe's cage a few feet from the window so he could see out and enjoy the view and the sun if he felt like warming himself. He had free flight in the room, so I kept the door shut all the time. My brother kept his door shut too, although I don't know why; he had nothing that would fly away.

One morning I heard him cry out! I scrambled out of bed and rushed to his door. It was shut and I could hear him crying while talking to someone. I knocked on his door, "Warren, are you okay?"

"Yes," he replied, "go way and leave me alone!"

I was not to be put off so easily. "Warren, what's wrong?" I stood there at his door waiting for a response. I could still hear him crying, but he was no longer talking to anyone. I probably shouldn't have done it, but I opened his door slightly and peeked in. He was lying in bed with the covers pulled over his head. I pushed the door open a little more and glanced around his room. What a mess; I had never seen anything like it!

"Warren, can I help? What's wrong?"

He pulled the covers slightly down so he could peek at me. "What are you doing? Get out of here," he screamed at me!

I had been so carried away by the disarray that I saw in his room, I totally forgot and didn't notice that I had inadvertently stepped into his room uninvited. I quickly backed out and offered my sincere apology. I explained that I was just worried about him. He reassured me that he was alright and said there was nothing to worry about. He had had a bad dream.

Later that day he told me that he had decided to start attending a church in Suquamish. He liked a girl that attended there and he was friends with some of her brothers and cousins. He said that his nightmare had been about them. In my mind I thought that that should have had been an omen or something to that effect, but I didn't think it was any of my business. I just pondered on it deeply; it bothered me that anyone would start going to particular church because they liked a certain person. I felt like our reasons for attending any church should be based on a higher cause.

I was still a devout Methodist even though I was not attending regularly anymore because of our move back to Fort Ward. Mom had brought me to a church in Winslow because the minister was Methodist, but I didn't feel comfortable there. I just would rather not go; I would be leaving in August anyway, so it didn't really matter very much to me.

My friend Cheryl and I had quite an adventure on the 4th of July. There was a street dance in Winslow, so we had made plans for her to spend the night at my house after attending the dance. At the dance, we met a couple of boys that were considerably older than us. One of them had a car and they offered to drive us home to Fort Ward. The hour was early; the fireworks would not have started for at least another couple of hours. It started out perfectly innocent, just two girls and two boys having a fun night out.

Needless to say, innocence doesn't last long when the boys are considerably older than the girls! On the way home, they stopped at the beach to park; they wanted to make-out! Neither Cheryl nor I had any experience in such behavior. I was just curious enough to want to kiss the guy I was with, but that's all I wanted to do. I let him kiss me and I kissed him back. Pretty soon, we were really kissing! I opened my eyes and looked in the back seat to see that Cheryl and the other boy were kissing as intensely as we were! I didn't want things to get out of hand, so I said, "We really shouldn't be doing this."

He pulled away and asked, "How old are you?" I said I was fourteen and he backed away as he said to his friend in the backseat, "They are only fourteen!"

That brought everything to an abrupt halt; they did not intend to get themselves or us into trouble! We proceeded to go home. As we entered through the old gate of the fort, the guy I was with said that he had never been up there. I started telling him about the Francis Nash Battery and some of the old buildings. We ended up taking a nighttime stroll through Francis Nash. He had a flashlight. However, it was so dark that we felt it was rather dangerous to be wandering through those old corridors. We left the battery and headed toward home.

As we were approaching the drive that led to my house, I pointed out the brick house on the corner. I told them about the woman that lived there whose name was Mrs. Broom. I described her as being an eccentric, old woman with red hair that fell to her knees. I told them that I imagined the woman as being a witch because of her name and the way she stood out on her porch in the morning, sweeping with her dilapidated broom while her long, red hair blew in the wind.

It was too much for those boys; they had to investigate the house. We parked the car down the street from the house and walked to the old, brick building. We tried to peer through the windows, but it was useless; we could not see in. I was sure that she wasn't home; she only came once in a while. I believed that she lived full-time in Seattle. The guy I was with said, "Let's go around to the back and see if we can find a way inside."

Now I was getting nervous; however, I was just as curious as he was. I looked at Cheryl and she just shrugged her shoulders. (I never dreamed that when I was an old woman, I would retell this story!) We tried the back door and of course, it was locked. Next, we went down some stairs that led to a basement door; it was locked too. Then to my utter dismay and shock, he broke the window! He reached in and opened the door. We went in; breaking and entering is what did!

We entered into a basement storage room. There were some very large crates; they looked just the right size to hold coffins! I'm sure that our imaginations were extremely heightened because of what we had done, but those boxes were perfectly shaped to hold coffins. I could not think of anything else that size and shape; I wanted out of there fast!

We scrambled out of there and quickly went back to the car. The guys drove us to my house and we said goodnight. It was also good-bye; we never saw them again. Cheryl and I went into the house. Mom was surprised to see us; I told her that we had met some guys who drove us home. She was fine with that; she didn't need to drive to Winslow and get us. Cheryl and I never told anyone what we had done on the night of the 4th.

Several days later, I was walking home from my friend Kitten's house, when a sheriff pulled up in his car. He rolled down his window and said, "Mrs. Broom had her house broken into a few days ago. Do you know anything about it?" I looked right at him and said, "No, it must have been some teenagers." He drove away, and I thought to myself, "I'm a very good actress!"

My problems with older boys continued! One day as I was walking home from Kitten's, a boy who was driving a red convertible, stopped to ask me directions. I told him how to get where he was going and he started to drive away. Then he backed up and said, "Why don't you show me how to get there?" I said that I needed to get home very soon because I had to make dinner for my family.

He said that he just had to drop this package off to a friend of his mother's and then he could bring me right home. I don't know if I was still just totally naïve, or if my desire to ride in a red convertible was too much for me to overcome, but like a fool, I said okay.

We drove on up to the corner of the fort where our old apartments were located. He dropped his package off at the house next door to where the people lived that would be giving me a ride to California. Luckily, they either were not at home, or at least not sitting out on their front porch; I did not want them to see me!

We then proceeded to drive back to my house. As he pulled up in front of the house, my little brothers came running over to admire his red convertible. The boy, who was only two years older than me, said that it was his car. I wondered if that were true, but I didn't want to appear to be nosy. He asked for my phone number and I gave it to him. He said that he would call me and he took off. He seemed harmless enough, and I thought I might like having him for a temporary boyfriend; nothing was going to get in my way of going to California!

True to his word, he called me that very night. We talked on the phone for quite a while, getting to know each other better. He ended the conversation by saying that he would come over the next day and we could figure out something to do for fun. I decided from that phone conversation that I now had a new boyfriend; did I ever have a lot to learn!

The next day, Mr. Convertible came over around 10:00 in the morning. It was a beautiful, summer day; the kind people daydream about. Mom was at work and the kids were all playing with their friends. There was a field of tall grass growing between the drive around our houses and the main road. Mr. Convertible said, "Let's go and play *Splendor in the Grass*."

"What?" was all I could manage to ask. I understood immediately what he wanted to do, and I wanted no part of it! I didn't want him to think I was afraid, so I said, "Someone will see us." He laughed and said no one could see us if we were lying down because the grass was at least four feet high. He said if we went out in the middle of the field, we would never be seen.

He was quite convincing, but for me, it was more than being afraid of being seen. I simply was not ready to give myself to some boy that I hardly knew. I had made up my mind a couple of years before that I was going to wait until I got married before I gave myself to a man. I don't know from where I summoned the courage or resolve to tell him, but I did. He looked at me and smiled and said, "Okay." I thought he would then drop me like a hot potato, but he surprised me and said, "Let's go to my house."

I told him that I was watching my younger siblings and that I couldn't leave. He asked when I would be able to go and see his house and meet his parents. I told him that I would be free on Saturday, and he said that he would be over to pick me up around 10:00. He drove away and I was left thinking, "He wasn't even upset with me; he might be an alright guy after all."

On Saturday morning, just as he said, he showed up promptly at 10:00 a.m. He met my mother and dad, and they were quite impressed by his red convertible. It was another beautiful day, but he said I may want to get a sweater because he had the top down and it was also rather windy out at the beach. Mom and I went into the house. I went upstairs to fetch a sweater and when I came down, Mom said, "I really don't know what that boy sees in you. He's obviously from a well-to-do family; you have no money and you're not pretty. I just don't see why he's even interested."

Mom had done it again. I don't know if she deliberately wanted to ruin my life, or if she just said things without thinking. Either way, the damage was done. I was miserable and spent the day feeling unsure about myself. I tried to put on a good act (more practice for being an actress) and pretend to be having a wonderful time.

Mr. Convertible's parents were not at home. He showed me around the downstairs of his house and then wanted to take me up to see his room. Oh brother! I suddenly realized that he knew that his parents would not be home. What a jerk; I just wanted him to take me home. I told him that I would like him to take me home. I lied and said that I had a headache; I had read that in many romance novels. He must have believed me or realized that he wasn't going to get his way with me because he said, "Let's go."

I was only too happy to go home. I then thought that I would share with Mom what Mr. Convertible thought he could get from me. To my complete shock, Mom thought there was nothing wrong with that! She just said, "Oh, I wondered what his interest in you was." I was convinced that going to California was not only a good idea, but necessary; I had plans for my life and saving myself for Mr. Right was one of them!

Mr. Convertible didn't give up! He suddenly appeared one day, perhaps a week after I had let him know that I wasn't interested in his obvious passion. Maybe he liked the idea of a challenge; he was undoubtedly spoiled and had what he wanted most of the time. He tried persuading me with every trick in the book; I wasn't going to fall for any of it. I told him he had wasted his time by coming over; I wasn't interested in him or his car. I would be leaving for California soon and that I hoped I would never see him again. I guess he finally got the message; he said good-bye, hopped in his car, and drove out of my life.

CHAPTER 25

GOOD-BYE

I was packed and ready to go; the fact that I wasn't leaving until Monday morning was of little consequence. It was Saturday and I had spent the better part of the morning packing and repacking my big, blue suitcase. I had very few clothes that I wanted to bring to California with me; most of them were either too worn, out of style, or much too warm for the climate. I had earned enough through my allowance to buy some new things when I got to Garden Grove.

I sadly moved Pepe downstairs into the breakfast nook. I wasn't sure just where to put him. I didn't want him to get lonely, nor did I want anyone to forget to feed and water him. He was such a sweet, little parakeet and I loved him dearly; I would miss him more than anyone or anything else from my crazy, mixed-up life. I would miss my best friend Cheryl, but not enough to give up my dream of becoming an actress, or for that matter, rescuing my father from the Mormons if it turned out that he needed to be rescued. So many thoughts were going through my head as I gently pet Pepe and gave him a quick, affectionate kiss. He certainly loved to be kissed; he would return my one kiss with dozens of his own. Sometimes he acted as though he wanted to climb into my mouth; he was such an adoring little friend.

My little sister, Susy was going to be hard to leave. I had wanted a baby sister so much; when she was born, I was filled with immense joy. We hadn't been close while she was growing up; there were six years between us and that made the relationship difficult. However, she was growing up and I was going away. Mom was telling everyone that I would be back in September for school, but I knew different. I was going to miss some really important years in Susy's life and it saddened me. There again, my feelings for my little sister were not enough to entice me to give up on my dreams.

My brother David, whose birthday was the day before mine, had grown up enough that I felt confident to leave the care of my younger siblings to him. Mom was gone at work enough that someone who had a sense of responsibility needed to be home to keep an eye on them. David would be turning twelve the day I left and I would be turning fifteen the next day.

Warren seemed happy for me; he kept telling me stories about Grandma and Grandpa Van Pelt. He also told me a few stories about other relatives that he had met but not gotten to know very well. He said that I would love California and probably would never want to come back to Washington. Warren had lived with our father in Los Angeles and was not familiar with Garden Grove or Orange County. However, he said that our father often reminisced about Garden Grove High School and the fun time he had had on their track team.

Mom was acting as though I would hate California and want to come home before the end of August. She was going to buy me a bus ticket when I was ready to come home and have it waiting for me at the Greyhound Terminal. The thought of riding a bus 1200 miles did not sound appealing since I tended to get carsick, but I knew that was all Mom could afford. It surprised me that she was being so supportive of my wanderlust. During a conversation we had that evening, I found out why!

Mom told me that my father had never once paid any child support for me or Warren. She had not expected any for my oldest brother Jerry because he was not my father's son. However, the terms of their divorce had stated that he owed monthly child support. He never paid a cent and Mom never asked for it. She felt sorry for him; she said that he went nuts after the divorce. She said that people saw him tossing clothes and things out his car window as he drove away from their house. He went back into active duty with the Navy, and she did not hear from him for several years. By then he had calmed down and accepted the fact that she had remarried.

When I had been such a sickly young child, she could have used some financial aid from him; I cost our family a lot of money. My stepdad never complained; he loved me like his own. However, Mom felt like me going to live with my father was an opportunity for him to have the responsibility of paying for some of my care. True, I was now in good health, but he could furnish other things to ease the finances of my cash-strapped family. He would be able to provide new clothes, shoes, perhaps some dental work, and whatever else I may need. It appeared that Mom had thought this out and that was why she was so willing to let me go.

I was surprised, to say the least. I had no idea that Mom had ever expected money from my father; I hadn't even thought about it. I knew that other kids got support from their fathers if their parents were divorced, but I thought it was just something they did out of love, not because it was a court order. I was really naïve about such matters.

Mom told me that my father would try to say he had no money to do this or that for me; he had always treated her in that way. However, he always had money to pay for his voice lessons or tuxedos to wear for his performances. He took himself out for his meals and brought his clothes to the cleaners; he had plenty of money, he just didn't want to spend it on anyone but himself.

I reminded her that he had provided nicely for Warren the years that he had lived with him. She said that Grandma and Grandpa, plus my great aunt had seen to it that Warren had the things he needed. If my father had not had them around, Warren would not have been so well provided for. She told me that because I was older than Warren had been, I was smart enough to take care of myself and to get my father to provide for me the way that he should.

Oh my goodness! Now I had more reasons to go and live with my father; I was helping out our family too! I hugged Mom and told her that I loved her. I reminded her that I planned to stay in California and attend high school there. She said not to make that decision until I had been there a while, but that in the meantime, get him to provide me with some of the items we had discussed. I promised that I would.

Sunday morning, August 9th, dawned clear and bright. The extended family was having a huge gathering out at Fay Bainbridge State Park. Normally on Sundays, we would all travel out to Twin Spits, but that day was a special day. Aunt Ariel was celebrating her birthday, David and I were celebrating ours, and I think a few other extended family members had August birthdays; plus, it was a good-bye for me.

As usual, for our Fay Bainbridge picnics, our family reserved the big shelter down on the beach. There were about 60 of us gathered that day. The Tribe family was there, in addition to some other family friends that often joined in on our Sunday gatherings. Several birthday cakes had been provided; I guess they wanted to make sure we all got an opportunity to blow out some candles.

Aunt Virginia and Aunt Ariel, in particular, wanted to discuss my going to California. Neither one of them could see the reason for me to leave my home here and go so far away. I loved my aunts so much and I did not want to make them sad, so I didn't want to say anything that may upset them. I knew that they would not be able to understand my reasons for going, especially about my father having just joined the Mormon Church. They were devout Methodists and if they knew that he had now become a Mormon, they would probably have been very fearful for me. If my Methodist minister believed that Mormons worshiped the Devil, then they probably believed it too. No, I couldn't share that information with them, nor could I tell them about the financial reasons I was going. If I said anything about our family's lack of money, both of them would probably have offered to let me live with them. As wonderful as that would have been, I could not have pursued my dream of becoming an actress.

I just smiled and said that I wanted to see California and get to know my other grandparents. I told them that if I didn't like it there or was homesick, I would take the Greyhound bus home and be back in time for school in September. When they asked what my parents thought of my little escapade, I said they had no objections. That was the end of the conversation; I thought!

Most everyone had been crowded into the shelter during this little conversation between my two aunts and me. When I ended the conversation and started to walk out of the shelter, the oldest Tribe boy stepped up to me and said, "Can we have a talk?" I had no idea what he wanted; I hadn't really talked to him since he had kissed me ten months earlier.

"I guess so," was all I could think to say. He invited me to sit inside his truck, out of the wind. The truck was parked directly in back of the shelter, in plain view of passersby, so I figured it was safe enough. He opened the passenger door for me and I climbed up and in. He went around to the other side, climbed in, and shut the door. I suddenly felt trapped and wished that I had not agreed to have a private, little chat with him. I braced myself, not knowing what he was going to say.

"Why do you have to go?" he whined. "I'm going to miss you so much!"

"Oh Brother," was all I could think, but I didn't say it! I didn't want to hurt his obviously tender feelings. I told him that I was sorry but that I really wanted to go to California. I told him that I wanted to try to get into acting somehow and that there were no opportunities for such things here on Bainbridge Island. In order for me to have any chance at all, I needed to be where the action was! I rambled on, stating my reasons, hoping to instill within him the fact that I no longer belonged on the island. I wanted him to see things my way so that he would be happy for me instead of feeling sorry for himself. I really didn't understand why he liked me, nor did I want him to; I still thought of him as more of a brother than a boy.

It became apparent to me that I was not going to convince him to change his perspective, so I abruptly ended the conversation. "I guess this is good-bye," was all I said, and I let myself out of the truck. I quickly walked up the hill to where the swings and slide were; I had memories from that playground that I had to put to rest.

The slide still looked the same as it did when I painfully slid down to please my mother at the second-grade picnic. I had had blood poisoning that morning and had to get a penicillin shot, and my bottom was so sore, I could hardly walk. She had insisted that I play, so I tried to please her and pretend to have fun. It was so painful that once I managed to slide down, I went back to the little shelter where our class was stationed and told Mom that I needed to go home. The sad memory of my teacher giving me my failing report card and telling me that I had been bad for not studying at home brought tears to my eyes.

I went over to the swings and sat down on my favorite one. I remembered how years earlier, my cousin Dolores had taught me how to pump so that I no longer had to rely on someone to push me. She had opened up a whole new experience for me; I loved to swing, the higher the better. I pushed off and started the familiar pump and pull. As I swung higher, my cares lifted, and I was carried away in happy thoughts as I looked down over the beach and the deep, blue water.

I could see Seattle in the distance, and I remembered all the times I had taken the ferryboat to go to the hospital. I had been such a sick little girl, and now I was so healthy. It seemed like a miracle to me that my life could change so drastically just from a simple tonsillectomy. As I swung higher, I felt the breeze on my face. I remembered how as a young child I would pretend that I could fly; I remembered pretending to be Peter Pan and how I would never grow up. Unfortunately, that was only pretend and I did grow up. I was going to be fifteen on Tuesday; I was growing up way too fast.

I stopped pumping the swing and let it slowly come to a gentle stop. I had considered jumping off while it was still in midair but decided against it because I didn't want to risk getting injured. That would have really put a damper on my plans! I walked down the hill and back to the noise and commotion within the shelter. Everyone was talking and laughing, simply enjoying being together. I knew that I was going to miss this wonderful extended family and joy I felt when I was with them.

Uncle Stanley walked into the shelter with a bundle of freshly carved sticks. He had been sitting out on a log, sharpening the ends of some willow sticks so that we could have the fun of roasting marshmallows. Yes indeed, he was the closest thing to the real Santa Claus I had ever known. As I watched him hand out sticks to all of the kids, I remembered when he and Aunt Virginia had taken me camping. They had also taken me out to Kaleloch on numerous occasions, and we had stayed in a cabin above the beach. I had lived with them for a semester while I was in the fifth grade. Of all my extended family, these two people were who I would miss the most. My thoughts and feelings for them were almost enough to persuade me to change my mind and not leave; however, I had a dream and I was not going to be deterred.

I roasted a marshmallow and gently slid the golden, outer crust off the sweet delicacy and popped it into my mouth. As I let is dissolve, I put the remaining marshmallow above the hot coals and let it plump up and roast to a nice, golden brown. Again, I popped the outer shell into my mouth. My marshmallow was only going to survive three rounds above the coals; the tiny remains puffed up and turned the perfect shade to pronounce it ready. Into my mouth it went, and I reached for another out of the bag.

The day lingered on into the evening; no one seemed the least interested in calling it a day and heading home. I certainly did not want the day to end; it was the best birthday I had had since I got my blue bike. That thought brought back a cascade of memories; I was making myself homesick, and I hadn't even left yet! The aunts began clearing off the tables and putting things away. Once the aunts got busy, the uncles took notice and hopped up and began to carry items out to their cars. Clearing away a huge picnic can be a lot of work. It's amazing how fast the work can be accomplished with so many hands helping. All of a sudden, it was time to say good-bye.

For everyone else, it was just the usual hug and good-bye until next weekend. However, for me, it became the most difficult good-bye I had as yet experienced. My aunts and uncles thought they were only hugging me to send me off on a month-long adventure. However, I was holding each of them a bit longer and with more intensity than I had ever done before; I was saying good-bye for heaven knew how long.

Monday morning I was up at the crack of dawn. I needed to be up so that I could say good-bye to Dad before he left for work. We hugged and I told him that I loved him. He had tears in his voice as he said, "I love you too and don't you forget it." He quickly went out the door, climbed into his car, and drove away. Good-byes are difficult for everyone, and right then I could tell that he was having a hard time; however, I couldn't let the emotions of the morning deter me from my plan.

Mom was up and asking if I wanted her to fix me some breakfast; that was odd since most of the time we just ate cold cereal. I told her no thank you and just grabbed a box of Cheerios; I figured that I needed some cheering just about then. I had barely finished eating when our friends showed up. Mom exclaimed her usual, "Oh My God!"

Suddenly Mom was filled with emotion; she was crying and so was I. We hugged really hard, as though we were saying good-bye for a lifetime. I pulled away and said, "I have to go." I grabbed my suitcase and a few other belongings and headed out the door.

Mr. James opened the back door of the car; my friend was sitting in the back seat anxiously waiting for me. She had made room amongst all her traveling gear for me and my little bit of home. She laughed when she saw my parka and said that I would not be needing that heavy jacket in Southern California. Her mom said that perhaps I may make a trip to the mountains or out to the beach at night when a warm jacket would be very welcome.

I rolled down the window to wave good-bye to Mom as we drove away. She was standing on the back porch, wiping tears from her eyes with one hand, while clinging to the railing with the other. As I watched, she sat down on the stairs to have a good cry and pulled out her cigarettes. I turned back toward the front of the car and thought, "California here I come, right back where I started from!"

EPILOGUE

Join Vicki as she leaves her island home and heads to California to begin a new life and fulfill her dreams. Experience with her the trials and triumphs of being a teenage girl in a new school, in a new state, and not knowing a single soul. Feel the thoughts and emotions as Vicki investigates the Mormon religion and eventually converts and embraces the Church of Jesus Christ of Latter-day Saints. Teen years should be fun, full of life, love, and learning. However, for Vicki, the path she chose was as different as the changing tide.

ABOUT THE AUTHOR

Victoria Farnsworth was born in California but grew up on a beautiful island in the Pacific Northwest. She spent three years in California as a teenager but returned to the Pacific Northwest to graduate from high school. It was during her senior year that she met her husband and after his return from Viet Nam, they married. They have been married for 45 years and together have three married daughters and eight beautiful (and highly intelligent) grandchildren. Due to health reasons, Victoria has moved to Payson and is enjoying her retirement surrounded by the natural beauty of the mountains in central Arizona.

She had her first work published in the Reader's Digest in August of 1983. She spent the next several years writing poems for family, friends, and church but never endeavoring to publish her work. She kept busy working as a secretary for the Department of the Navy for several years. She then spent the next 15 years teaching swimming and related aquatic classes for various school and park districts in the states of Washington, Oregon, and California.

During her years working outside the home, she was also busy raising a family of three girls. As is every mother, she was busy driving girls to lessons, sports, and church activities. She had to deal with teenage boys, lovesick girls, and being married to a millworker turned truck driver.

When the girls all left home for school or marriage, rather than feel like an empty nester, she spent time in serious prayer and contemplation. She then embarked on a new career path and became Clara the Clown. Seven years were spent clowning around up and down the West Coast. As always, she was busy with church service and managed to be a Relief Society President during this time. Her new career ended when a car accident forced her to retire. After becoming a Master Gardener she started a new business doing landscape design. Unfortunately, another car accident forced her to once again give up something she loved.

Writing continued to be a hobby. During her 10 year membership in the Glove & Trowel Garden Club, she spent 4 years as secretary and writing the quarterly update of the club's activities. In June of 2011 Victoria had an article published in the Northwest Landscape Professional magazine about butterfly gardening. So many people read the article and commented that she should write professionally; a seed was planted! Victoria kept an online journal of her life in Mexico and continues with a website devoted to her new life and home in Payson, Arizona: http://victoriafarnsworth.weelby.com. She also has a website devoted to her writing and books: http://liveanextraordinarylife.weebly.com/

One book could not begin to hold 60 plus years of unforgettable events; hence this work will take many volumes to tell the story of the extraordinary life of an ordinary woman.

Made in the USA
San Bernardino, CA
10 April 2015